CREATING NEW LIFE, NURTURING FAMILIES

Creating New Life, Nurturing Families

A

WOMAN'S

PERSPECTIVE

Sidney Callahan

ST. ANTHONY MESSENGER PRESS
Cincinnati, Ohio

Scripture passages have been taken from *New Revised Standard Version Bible*, copyright ©1989 by the Division of Christian Education of the National Council of the Churches of Christ in the U.S.A., and used by permission. All rights reserved.

Book and cover design by Mark Sullivan
Cover image © istockphoto.com/Pieter Bregman

LIBRARY OF CONGRESS CATALOGING-IN-PUBLICATION DATA

Callahan, Sidney Cornelia.
Creating new life, nurturing families : a woman's perspective / Sidney Callahan.
 p. cm. — (Called to holiness : spirituality for Catholic women)
Includes bibliographical references and index.
ISBN 978-0-86716-893-8 (pbk. : alk. paper) 1. Catholic women—Religious life. I. Title.
BX2353.C35 2009
248.8'431—dc22
 2009026606

ISBN 978-0-86716-893-8

Copyright ©2009, Sidney Callahan. All rights reserved.

Published by St. Anthony Messenger Press
28 W. Liberty St.
Cincinnati, OH 45202
www.SAMPBooks.org
www.CalledtoHoliness.org

Printed in the United States of America.

Printed on acid-free paper.

09 10 11 12 5 4 3 2 1

CONTENTS

ABOUT THE SERIES | *vii*

PREFACE | *ix*

CHAPTER ONE: *Family, Marriage and Parenting as Daring Venture* | *1*

CHAPTER TWO: *Love* | *13*

CHAPTER THREE: *Marriage* | *21*

CHAPTER FOUR: *Sexuality* | *43*

CHAPTER FIVE: *Mothering* | *55*

CHAPTER SIX: *Women and Work* | *75*

CHAPTER SEVEN: *Suffering, Joy and Transformation* | *101*

NOTES | *119*

BIBLIOGRAPHY | *119*

INDEX | *121*

ABOUT THE SERIES

I wish to acknowledge the support and encouragement of an organization of philanthropists: Foundations and Donors Interested in Catholic Activities (FADICA). In January of 2005, I was invited to speak before this organization at a conference entitled Women of Faith. The discussion explored the many contributions of women to Roman Catholic ministry, church leadership and theology.

The members of FADICA heard my appeal for a renewed focus on women's spirituality in the context of significant religious change during the twentieth century and the pressing challenges of the twenty-first. The need for a creative, solidly grounded and theologically sophisticated spirituality available in an accessible form for all Christian women seemed obvious. Follow-up conversations by the FADICA board, ably led by Frank Butler, led to a proposal from Fairfield University for a series of books on women's spirituality. Thus, FADICA, Fairfield University and St. Anthony Messenger Press formed a collaborative partnership to produce seven volumes under the title *Called to Holiness: Spirituality for Catholic Women*.

I wish to thank the individuals and foundations whose generosity made this collaborative venture possible. These include the Amaturo Family Foundation, the AMS Fund, the Cushman Foundation, the Mary J. Donnelly Foundation, George and Marie Doty, Mrs. James Farley, the Robert and Maura Burke Morey Charitable Trust, Maureen O'Leary, Ann Marie Paine and the Raskob Foundation for Catholic Activities. I wish to extend a word of thanks and praise to the entire FADICA membership, whose conscientious, quiet and loving participation in shaping the life of the church has been an inspiration.

PREFACE

The focus of this series is spirituality. Its interest is women of all back-grounds: rich and poor; married and single; white, black and brown; gay and straight; those who are biological mothers and those who are mothers in other senses. There will be volumes on grassroots theology, family life, prayer, action for justice, grieving, young adult issues, wisdom years and Hispanic heritage. I hope all the volumes in this series will deepen and shape your own spiritual life in creative ways, as you engage with the theology of our rich, two-thousand-year-old Christian tradition.

Women's spiritualities are lived in light of their concrete, specific experiences of joy and struggle; ecstasy and despair; virtue and vice; work and leisure; family and friends; embodiment and sexuality; tears and laughter; sickness and health; sistering and mothering. These volumes are for women and men from all walks of life, whether they are new to the spiritual journey or old hands, affluent, middle-class or poor. Included in the circle we call church are persons from every country on the planet, some at the center, others at the margins or even beyond.

The time is ripe for "ordinary" women to be doing theology. The first and second waves of the women's movement in the nineteenth and twentieth centuries provided a valiant and solid foundation for the third wave which will mark, and be marked by, the world of the early twenty-first century. Changes and developments from one generation to the next makes our heads spin. Younger women readers are likely to be already grooming the soil for a fourth wave of Christian spirituality done by and for women. Women have always loved God, served others and struggled with sin, but the historical context has been less than friendly in terms of women's dignity, acknowledgment of female gifts and empowerment by church and society. In a time of growing emphasis on the role of clergy, and the backlash against women in society, the voices of the laity—especially the voices of women—are needed more than ever.

The Greek language has two words for time. *Chronos* points to the time signaled by the hands on the clock—for example, it is a quarter past two. *Kairos* points to time that is ripe, a moment pregnant with possibility. As Christian women, we live in a time rightly described as *kairos*. It is a time that calls us, demands of us renewed energy, reflection and commitment to attend to and help each other grow spiritually as we seek to love ourselves and the world. At this point in history, the fruit of women's struggle includes new self-awareness, self-confidence and self-respect. More and more women are beginning to see just how lovable and capable they are. The goal of the Christian life has always been to lay down our lives in love for the other, but the particular ways this vocation is lived out differ from era to era and place to place. Women's ability to voice with confidence the phrase, "I am a theologian" at the beginning of the twenty-first century means something it could not have meant even fifty years ago.

Those who were part of the early waves of feminism celebrate the hard-won accomplishments of the women's movement and know that this work needs to be taken up by future generations. Young women in their twenties and thirties are often unaware of past efforts that brought about more dignity and freedom for women. Women have opened many doors, but many remain closed. The media have recently explored the plight of Hindu widows in India; less publicized is that women in the United States still earn only seventy-seven cents for every dollar earned by their male counterparts. We must be vigilant and continue to act for decades to come in order to secure our accomplishments thus far and make further inroads toward the creation of a just, egalitarian world. Those who sense that the women's movement is in a doldrums inspire us to renew the enthusiasm and dedication of our foremothers.

When we cast our eye beyond the women of our own nation, it takes but a split-second to realize that the majority of the world's poor and oppressed are women. A quick visit to the Women's Human Rights Watch Web site reveals the breadth and depth of women's oppression across the globe from poverty and domestic abuse to sex slavery. Most women (and their children) do not have enough to eat, a warm, dry place to sleep or access to education. Female babies are more at risk than male babies. Women, more than men, lack the protection of the law and the respect of their communities. The double-standard in sexual matters affects women in harmful ways in all cultures and economic groups across the globe.

For all of these reasons it is not just important—but pressing, crucial, urgent—that all women of faith own the title "theologian" and shape this role in light of each woman's unique set of characteristics, context, relationships and spiritualities. We are theologians when we sort through our experience and the great and small problems of our time through reflection on Scripture or the words of a mystic or theologian. The images of God that emerged for Paul, Augustine or Catherine of Siena provide guidance, but their theology cannot ever be a substitute for our own. Theology helps us shape what we think about God, justice, love, the destiny of humanity and the entire universe in a way that is relevant to the specific issues facing us in the twenty-first century. The call to spiritual depths and mystical heights has never been more resounding.

Elizabeth A. Dreyer
Series Editor

CHAPTER ONE

• FAMILY, MARRIAGE AND PARENTING
AS DARING VENTURE •

When women choose to marry and have children, they start on a daring venture. It takes courage to commit mind, body and heart to another person and to found a family in which the labors, joys, risks and struggles remain unknown. Yet the dramatic quality of a woman's leap into the future can remain as invisible as the air we breathe. Perhaps we do not attend because marrying and having children is so basic to human survival. Always and everywhere a new generation must be successfully conceived, borne and reared to adulthood, or humanity grinds to a halt. Countless acts of female altruism keep the world moving into the future.

I remember how my eyes were opened in those first weeks when I came home from the hospital with our newborn son. For the first time I realized that *every* adult I saw walking around on the street or in the grocery store was there because a woman had carried him or her in her womb for nine months, gone through childbirth and then, for a decade or more, proceeded to feed, diaper, clothe, soothe and vigilantly protect and instruct the child. This flash of insight was like the moment in the *Wizard of Oz* when the black-and-white picture bursts into color.

Having a baby after falling in love and experiencing sexual love revealed the hidden emotional depths undergirding the conventional world of daily routines. All of my feelings increased in intensity—I could be exalted, ecstatic, anxious and exhausted in turn. Anxiety appeared: Could I live up to the challenge of love and responsibility?

Huge reservoirs of female energy and labor are continually expended to nurture communal living. So why is this important work of caretaking discounted, while acclaim for human achievement regularly begins, "Let us now praise famous men?" Women who are creating and sustaining new life remain anonymous and unsung.

Women Are Cocreators With God
With deeper insight it becomes clear that nothing is more crucially important than creating new life and sustaining human families. When a woman becomes a wife and mother she directly imitates God, the creator and sustainer of new life. God's love is maternal, for it creates and nurtures all the astounding diversity of the world, both visible and invisible. Those feminist theologians who speak of God as Mother and name God "She Who Is" are giving voice to traditional Christian insights. God as ever creative Wisdom continually moves to bring new human life into being; God is rightly praised as "The Divine Liveliness." Drawing forth the evolving world into each emerging moment of time reveals God as "the Absolute Future," in whom and toward whom we move. How wonderfully the Divine Energy wells up in an ever flowing fountain of creativity. "See, I am making all things new" (Revelation 21:5). With God everything is filled with surprise and joy.

Christian women rejoice in the way the work of God as Holy Spirit enkindles, enlivens, enlightens and quickens reality. God's power emerges in a special way in human minds and hearts. Over billions of years of evolution, human consciousness and self-awareness has increased in capacity. We can receive and share God's love and life in a privileged way. With an inner consciousness and psychological awareness, we can be transformed into new creatures able to know, love and enjoy God. All people can be included in God's family, which is a communion of justice, love and mercy.

Indeed, Christ's disciples are called by him to continue his work and be cocreators of the new world coming to fulfillment. As the firstborn of many spiritual brothers and sisters, Jesus Christ gives God's power and life to the faithful so that they can become like God in their love and work. Christian women are cocreators in a special way when they marry and create families that aspire to participate in the divine community. But this challenge can seem overwhelming for ordinary self-centered individuals so focused on our own survival.

Wives and mothers in the midst of the arduous effort find themselves pleading to God for help: "God, give me the strength to love others as Christ loves us." Or, in hard-pressed moments of desperation, the stark plea may become: "Please God, be my anchor, hold me fast from harming these people I am committed to." Husbands and children can inspire incredible passions of love, but they may also provoke frustration and flaring moments of anger. Once I met a benign religious man who told me that he had never in his life felt a moment of hatred for anyone. Immediately, I knew that he had never been married or lived in a family raising children. Those on the front lines in the battle against empathy fatigue cannot avoid lapses and failure. Repentant spouses and parents are forced to recognize their dependence on God's Spirit for strength to stay the course.

The gifts and fruits of the Holy Spirit are the salvation of family life. Only through opening the self to God as enkindling Spirit can believers live in God's loving kindness. The fruits of the Holy Spirit described by Saint Paul in the New Testament (Galatians 5:22–23) are love, joy, peace, patience, kindness, generosity, faithfulness, gentleness and self-control. This is an attractive list. Who would not desire to have a husband or child like this? Who wouldn't want to be this kind of wife and mother? Families and communities who are able to live out these ideals, even in small increments, will abound in happiness. The old English word *engodded* describes persons transformed by God's Spirit and sets the Christian goal for every believer. The engodded person will be another Christ for each person encountered—especially those at home.

Becoming Transformed Together

How can ordinary Christians receive the promised fruits and dynamic energy of the Spirit to be transformed in their daily lives? The Spirit's gifts of courage and wisdom galvanize and guide right action and prudent decisions through inward prayer, but no one can be a Christian alone. Human beings are relentlessly social and are always formed and tutored by group life. The strength and love of faithful others allow us not only to survive but to develop physically, mentally and spiritually. Effective spiritual power is channeled through a family and community of faith. Group support is necessary to survive spiritually in an imperfect world that is always changing.

First we are drawn to those who give us the word and convey the good news. Then through attentive listening, understanding deepens. Only in the give and take of conversation and dialogue can we grow and develop. Living with our evolved dispositions for self-assertion, competition and selfishness (the opposite of our evolved altruism), humans need others to help them be good. Only others can free us from self-deception. Those we live with are the best sources for learning to see ourselves as others see us. Different generations in a family readily point out wider perspectives we should consider, but no one is as effective in critique of their elders as adolescents. Their newfound capacities for abstract reasoning are gleefully put into practice in the family. Through painful and positive exchanges, we learn. Only with and through others can we grow up, or grow kind and humble.

Cynics resist the message of human interdependence. "Hell is other people," wrote existentialist philosopher Jean Paul Sartre. Others assert that life is "nasty, brutish and short." Nothing much should be expected in an indifferent, cruel and meaningless world. For pessimists, every individual is on her or his own, mercilessly subject to the dark miseries of life. By contrast, Christians believe that the light has come and shines forth in their midst. No believer will deny the existence of evil, sin and suffering in the world, but even now God's saving power of love is overcoming all. Jesus said, "But take courage; I have conquered the world!" (John 16:33). God's power is the power of self-giving humility and love that unites with humanity. Heaven begins here on earth with other people.

In marriage and family faithful persons slowly and painfully grow up together into Christ. A second birth or renewed creation of self takes place through the power of the Holy Spirit. The emerging transformed Christian believer is able to grow in love of God and give love to others as to oneself. Loving and giving become second nature, producing the fruits of joy and peace. Engaging in each day's ordinary tasks, as well as in larger and more daring ventures, Christians steadfastly journey together toward their goal. Little by little, the Holy Spirit quickens and moves the faithful to become more like God. The great truth is fulfilled: God becomes human so that humans can become like God. The human being fully alive manifests God's glory. Truth to tell, it's actually the case that the measure you give is the measure you receive (Mark 4:24; Luke 6:38). Disciples receive their promised abundance of life and joy.

Joys and Challenges of Family Life: Diversity, Unity and Change
Christians understand God as One in Three Persons who is perpetually loving, giving and receiving. This Trinitarian view declares that interpersonal relationships are the fundamental ground of all reality. Why is there something rather than nothing? We and the universe are here because the Triune God's dynamic self-giving love overflows in creativity. God exemplifies the self-diffusion of all goodness. Light radiates outward and love desires the other's fullness of life. Uniqueness and variety, difference and otherness are valued in God's world which brings them together in one love. Families love the uniqueness of each of their members as well as the bonds that tie them together as a family. Since human beings are made in the image of the Divine Liveliness, they are constantly growing and changing. Infants and adolescents in particular seem to grow before your eyes every day, but persons at every

age are moving through time and responding to ever-changing environmental conditions.

There is a dynamic movement in the complex dance of each marriage and of every family group. Sometimes it is difficult to see what is truly happening. The different dancers do their own thing, but also interweave their steps and rhythms in concert with others. No wonder the reality of relationships is so hard for us to comprehend and appreciate.

What is a marriage like? What makes a family? Every participant has her or his distinctive viewpoint which itself is constantly changing. Human self-awareness evolves as we progress through different seasons of development. The simplest conversation between two people consists of thousands of simultaneously changing actions and reactions as varying signals and cues are sent and received. In addition, nonverbal, subconscious channels of communication complement language. Quicksilver responses on multiple wavelengths are the order of the day in human interchanges. Certainly conscious, explicit linear events take place, but in and around them intuitive instant parallel processes are operating. Think of the way a magnet's force field creates a pattern of movements in a group of iron filings.

The incredible complexity and diverse layers of relationships surely help explain why we experience life as abundant and engaging. Interacting with any individual stimulates us, but being with those we love delights us and refreshes our spirits. Being together makes us feel good. Simply by living and breathing, loved ones challenge us to change. When women think about love, marriage, children and family life, it is important to reflect on the ecology of influences unique to each marriage and family. There is always an emotional atmosphere—a prevailing weather system—in operation. Mary Poppins isn't the only one sensitive to the wind changing. Unfortunately, cold fronts and chilling ice storms can arrive. Things may fall apart in rapid order or disintegrate slowly.

On the bright side, the constant movements of human beings provide the potential for new and creative responses that shape the future. A loving word or gesture heads off a squall. Harmful conditions can be avoided and grievous wounds healed. Unexpected reconciliations take place in an open future. A marriage, a family, the whole of a life story is never over and finished. Hope springs from the dynamic openness and potential surprises God makes possible.

Practicing Love
When wives and mothers resolve to imitate Christ and love God and neighbor, they may discover that their neighbor in need is not encountered primarily in a rare emergency on the road to Jericho, but right at home. Day and night, women are on call, constantly oriented and alert to the needs of their families. When Christian women follow the gospel ideal of laying down their lives for their friends, the friends in question are often kith and kin. Laying down our lives does not usually mean martyrdom, but it is always concrete. Marriage and family life mean a lifetime of altruistic, personally attentive work. Love's labor is never lost in the constant round of physical and psychological acts of care.

At a conference last year, I was asked to respond to a paper that describes new research indicating that the way families eat dinner together and tell family stories positively affects the children's future development. The paper's findings moved me to thought. I calculated that I had cooked well over twenty thousand dinners in more than fifty years of family life—and still counting. And what about those thousands of conversations? What role had they played in the shaping of our family story?

As a result of this consciousness-raising encounter, I resolved never, ever again to complain about cooking dinner. I also recommitted myself to engage in conversation at meals with my husband, resident granddaughter or guests. The paper also stimulated me to the rueful reflection that time spent cooking and eating is but a fraction of the work needed to keep a modern family up and running. Never mind laundry, shopping, cleaning, going to the bank or library, and driving to and from school and other events. Just keeping track of everyone's whereabouts, appointments and trips can crowd the memory bank.

Middle-class American women are blessed in their material and technological resources for family living, but standards also keep rising. As circumstances become more complex, choices increase; leisure and enrichment activities proliferate. Affluent women can find themselves as harassed and burdened with tasks as earlier, poorer generations of women. A cottage industry has grown up to help women cope and lower stress levels. With each new choice, women end up adding yet more activities to their already full schedules. Deciding to stop and assess our lives and relationships becomes a priority.

As women become increasingly aware of the importance of relationships, there is a corresponding increase in their appreciation of the concrete effects of love and positive emotions in marriage and family life. Dozens of books have been published in the last decades on happiness and how to become happy. Thus a woman's expectations for marriage and childrearing have increased along with other standards of living. But then, how could it not? With the acceptance of women's equal rights, dignity and opportunities for education and work, some women come into marriage on an equal footing with men. Communication can be easier between similarly empowered and educated men and women. When the status gap is closed, there is more potential for supportive and cooperative friendship in marriage. More married people report that their spouse is their best friend.

People regularly report that their family is their greatest source of happiness. Does this mean that certain benign cultural winds are beginning to blow? Loving and giving love begets joy and satisfaction. Good things do happen to good people. Those who help others out of intrinsic motivation are happier. Moreover, mutual self-giving sexual love is valued for the increase in love and pleasure it brings.

Although we cannot deny the level of cultural selfishness, domestic and child abuse and other social ills, modern culture values altruism and the giving and receiving of love. While women's work to create life and sustain families is still undervalued, wives and mothers lay claim to happiness and spiritual satisfactions. Great numbers of women join the increasing number of support groups centered on spirituality, study and self-help. Optimistic cultural critics rightly claim that these movements witness to a rising consciousness of life's goodness. Many of us have taken part in an exercise that involves creating a gratitude list—an overwhelmingly female activity.

Women are sustained by faith, liturgy and Scriptures as well as the praises and thanksgiving they offer to God. "My spirit magnifies the Lord," exults Mary, for "God has done great things for me." Mary's courageous response to God's invitation is her leap of faith and the most daring of ventures into the unknown. She does not hesitate to question how such an event can be, but then makes her great act of trust. "Let it be done unto me according to thy word." So begins the good news, the greatest story ever told.

Just as women create gratitude lists and join spiritual groups, we excel in organizing our celebrations and joyful occasions. Holidays and feasting are forms of high play that keep civilizations going. Families celebrate milestones together and women mostly manage the events. It is the rare man who has planned and executed his child's fourth birthday party. Beyond the commercialization and excess of holidays, an important value glimmers. This year I may have been happy to delegate decorating my fiftieth-something Christmas tree, but having fifteen of my immediate family members (and three dogs) to dinner made me exceedingly glad.

The daring promise of love and marriage may be a high-risk venture, but the harvest can be bountiful. The mustard seed grows into a large tree in which birds can nest. Even though they face the sorrows of the world, women relying on the help of the Spirit develop the patience and generosity to live with joy. The changing circumstances of our lives in the twenty-first century require that we think differently about spirituality. In future chapters we will dig more deeply into various dimensions of women's journeys. We discuss love and marriage, sex, mothering, work and transforming joy amidst suffering.

Food for Thought

1. Consider the scriptural list of the fruits of the Spirit and take time to reflect upon each one (Galatians 5:22–25). Where in your life do these spiritual and emotional qualities appear?
2. Where in your family life have you experienced healing? What positive surprises have you encountered in your spiritual journey?
3. Recall the self-giving practices of women in your family. Reflect on those times when you were successful in giving love to others, and those times when you failed. What made the difference?
4. As you think of your own journeys into the future you can benefit from looking at your past and the people who have formed you as a woman. Make a list of heroines in your life. Reflect on why you were attracted to them at the time and why you were drawn to admire other women's lives later. Did your religious education and spiritual experiences influence your choices?
5. Create a short gratitude list and take a moment to dwell on each item in prayer.
6. Society offers conflicting opinions on feminism. Reflect on any reading, conversations or arguments you may have had about women's nature and role in life. Name one of your strongest convictions on this topic and explain your position. What further questions do you still have?

Prayer

Invocation:
> Spirit of Life and Love
> > fill us with joy and hope
>
> Spirit of Life and Love
> > enkindle us to fiery generosity
>
> Spirit of Life and Love
> > confirm us in peace.

Scripture: Revelation 21:3–5

Response:
Let us pray for the power to be giving in love and patience:
> We trust in God our Future.

Let us pray for joy and gratitude:
> We trust in God our Future.

Let us pray for courage to be cocreators of the new:
> We trust in God our Future.

Prayer:
Christ our saving Lord, help us to grow in wisdom and love. We seek to be worthy of your promises and friendship. Help us to be patient and kind even when provoked and fatigued. In the busy routines of our lives let us cultivate gentleness and peace. Give us the grace to be generous and joyful. God, Our Mother, we thank you for bringing us into life and nurturing our growth. Amen.

CHAPTER TWO

• LOVE •

Love is praised in all times and all places. Nothing else inspires such heartfelt awe, joy and passionate deeds. No wonder that poetry, drama, novels, music, philosophy, religion and science perennially try to understand the mysterious nature of love. What is this thing called love? Does love really make the world go round or move the heavens and the stars? Women who fall in love, marry for love and love their children do well to ponder the depth of the drama of love they enact upon life's stage.

Christians clearly make astounding claims about the nature of love. Scripture tells us that God is love, and where love is, God is (1 John 4:7-8). The core of the good news is that God so loves the world that God in Christ comes to save it (John 3:16–17). Jesus as God's Word comes to bring his brothers and sisters into God's eternal family life of love. The life, death and resurrection of Jesus enables human beings to share in God's love and liveliness, here and now, and forever more.

Jesus tells his disciples that all of the law is fulfilled by the command to love God with all your heart and mind and strength, and your neighbor as yourself. But the great love commandment stirs up questions and doubts in us. How can this kind of love be practiced by ordinary men and women?

All too obviously, failures of love continue to mar the human story and fuel the plots of soap operas, novels, poems and popular songs. The obstacles and the distortions of love are as puzzling as they are distressing. When the Beatles chant their refrain "love, love, love" and go on to insist that "Love is all you need," they ignore perplexing complications. Christian claims for love and the great love commandment challenge the mind's understanding as well as the heart's strength. How am I supposed to love God, my neighbor and myself? Are there different kinds of love?

In English we use one word—*love*—for all the different experiences of love and many Western thinkers have found this misleading. C.S. Lewis, the great Christian apologist of the last century, wrote of the traditional division of love into four distinct activities. First there is a godly kind of charity which is unconditional and is called *agape*. Then there is erotic love and desire, or *eros*, which is most typically seen in sexual love. Love of friends, or *philia* is seen as different from the first two and in turn is different from *storge*, or affection for familiar things. While these are all called "love" they should be differentiated, according to Lewis. Some theologians also distinguish the love of God from love of neighbor, and see both as opposite from the love of self.

Yet there is another way to think about love. In my view it is better to see love as essentially one in all of its incarnations. Certainly theologians now emphasize that love of God cannot be separated from love of neighbor; Scripture proclaims clearly that to love the invisible God you must love the neighbor that you can see. If not, you are a liar. Conflict between love of God and neighbor does not really make sense because God is not another super object or thing out there somewhere, but is the ground of all being, all becoming and all loving. The God of love makes loving possible.

In my experience the activity of loving appears essentially the same whether as wife, mother, sister, daughter, friend, student or disciple. Love of God or love of my child share the passion of marital love while love of my husband is suffused with maternal nurturing, charity, friendship and familiar affection. The unconditional self-giving of erotic sexual love is intermingled with maternal care, gentle courtesy and playfulness. Doesn't an upsurge of joy and delight mark all loving activity?

A WOMAN'S PERSPECTIVE

Love of my children includes appreciation and passionate desire for their well-being.

Here we can gain support from the new evidence that the calming and happiness-inducing hormone oxytocin is released both in sexual intercourse and when nursing a baby. What a surprise it was for me to find that nursing can bring pleasure! Quite concretely in this case, erotic unions and maternal nurturing are producing similar joy. Yes of course love can fluctuate in its flames of intensity and differ in its appropriate expression; love can also be mixed with varied thoughts and emotions. In the case of more global kinds of loving, as in love of music, art or intellectual effort, many ideas accompany the loving but it still invokes passionate intensity and contented delight.

So what is the essence of love? I know it's truly love when I can say yes, yes and yes again to who or what I love, and embrace the loved person or activity with a heightened aliveness and commitment. The beloved is uniquely valued as an end, not a means to an end. My love is not aimed at some utilitarian goal. I am not loving my child or my husband in order to improve their personal social skills or to achieve some personal emotional high. Nor am I keeping an account in order to be paid back with equivalent favors. I am not trying to improve my "good girl" rating or holiness score. When I love, I simply accept, value and unite myself with the beloved, for now, in this present moment and forever.

Human consciousness has the amazing ability to go forth beyond the individual's boundaries in space and time to intertwine and unite with the other. When I join my mind and heart with the other I am enlarging and expanding myself into a new wholeness. The "I" becomes a "we." In love individuals become entwined, interconnected and intermingled. In love I feel safe and sound, in seeking I have found.

My loving makes me want to preserve the goodness and value of what I love. I desire to protect and take care of the loved one from this moment forward; fidelity and commitment arise naturally in loving.

CREATING NEW LIFE, NURTURING FAMILIES

Constancy is the mark of true love, or as Shakespeare's great sonnet proclaims: love is "an ever fixed mark…it is the star to every wandering bark… Love is not love which alters when it alteration finds."

Saint Paul's great scriptural discourse on love in 1 Corinthians 13:4–8 describes love's essential constancy and nurturing care. Paul writes,

> Love is patient; love is kind; love is not envious or boastful or arrogant or rude. It does not insist on its own way; it is not irritable or resentful; it does not rejoice in wrongdoing, but rejoices in the truth. It bears all things, believes all things, hopes all things, endures all things.
>
> Love never ends.

Human survival is made possible by parental altruism, strong ties and group loyalties. Ancient human remains show evidence of burial rites, and altruistic care of the old. Sharing food and nurturing the young and vulnerable are marks of humanity, along with cooperation and self-sacrificial defense of the group. Granted, aggressive competition within and between groups also exist as part of the human struggle, but evolution is not about the violent survival of the fittest, much less a war of all against all. Rather chance, competition and selection, play a necessary role in the emergence of new life forms. From the first appearance of life on earth there has been a progressive movement toward ever-greater complexity, consciousness and intelligence. Gene mutations, along with environmental events affect the survival of those organisms best adapted to the prevailing conditions. The chance impact of asteroids, the occurrence of epidemics and climate changes have affected the course of evolution.

In addition to chance and competition the operations of cooperation, love and altruism are seen as decisive. Cooperation and symbiosis allow individual cells to get together in new, more complex, mutually beneficial systems. New forms of life are built up and form new wholes. And the most astoundingly complex of all evolved phenomena on earth is the human body and brain built up of fifty billion cells interconnected and organized into systems that work together.

Having been built up slowly over the eons, the complex multidimensional systems of human beings do not work with perfect efficiency, but they are wondrously effective. *Homo sapiens* has evolved with the gift of language and is a prolific culture-maker. Adaptive functioning is increased in power by the invention of new tools and ways of life. From agriculture to writing, from religion to law, from medicine to the Internet, cultural evolution builds upon itself through the transmission of information over time and space.

Altruism and cooperation make it possible for new knowledge to be transmitted through the family and group. With intelligence and language come the ability to learn, to communicate and adapt to new circumstances. Cultural evolution is far speedier than the slower intergenerational genetic processes of evolution. The last seventy years have seen amazing cultural and technological changes. Religious understandings also are constantly evolving and developing through time.

Science and evolutionary psychology have thrown new light on the traditional Christian belief that humans are constantly on pilgrimage moving toward God's future. In an ever-changing world and within an ever-reforming church, embodied humans beings are cocreating God's dynamic creation. The claim that God's creative love is constantly at work becomes more apparent when we know that humans have evolved from the simplest forms of life to their present complexity. One appropriate image envisions the universe's initial Big Bang as the opening salvo of a divine symphony which is proceeding to play itself out through time, with new themes entering and combining in more complex movements and livelier tempos.

In this newly revised human evolutionary story, the positive emotions of love, joy and interest play as decisive a part as the unique human gifts of rationality, language and free will. With multiple kinds of human intelligences, humans can rationally imagine the future, predict effects from causes and choose between alternatives. But superior problem-solving, free agency and flexible behaviors are active because humans are also the most richly emotional of all species. In order to employ intelligence and capacities for invention, human beings must *want* to act, and *desire* to solve problems and explore new terrain. Without love, emotional desire, curiosity, interest and joy, who would care enough to be creative and inventive? Who could enjoy and celebrate their flourishing?

In fact, emotions and logic constantly interact. Thoughts arise and stimulate emotions, emotions engender thoughts and both induce actions which produce more ideas and feelings. When we look within we can observe the complicated ebb and flow of different kinds of consciousness. Memories, interactions with others, problem-solving, projections about the future and most often, desires, hopes and loves, are constantly intermingling.

Out of this complex system, a unique human consciousness emerges. Other primates and intelligent animals display emotional bonds and problem solving; they are conscious in the present, and act toward immediate goals; but humans are self-aware: we are conscious of being conscious. This self-awareness is the bedrock of all human thinking, loving and acting. When the philosopher Descartes said, "I think, therefore I am," he should have added, "And I am an *I* because I have been loved." The *I* has been created from the care of parents and others, who teach us what it means to be human.

We are innately loving altruists as well as competitors struggling for survival and status. Self-giving can produce joy. But is this really a surprise for Christians? Scripture asserts that it is more blessed to give than to receive. Jesus' beatitudes promise that happiness comes through loving God and others. We find ourselves by losing ourselves for God's sake. We receive in the measure we give.

Despite our belief in this idea, and our experience of its truth, in the midst of our daily struggles, it is easy to choose self-interest before love of others. A strong desire for some immediate gratification too often overpowers our commitment to long-term goals.

Of course, we are all differently equipped and prepared for love. Those who suffer early neglect or abuse do not easily trust in love or a future reward. Some genetic disorders, accidents and diseases can damage the brain and impair emotional health. Addiction and immaturity can bring chaos. Stress, illness, economic hardship and conflict can produce empathy fatigue and deplete our willpower. Each of us comes to adulthood with a unique history of weaknesses and wounds that need to be healed by love. No matter where we start, though, growing in love is a lifelong goal and the responsibility of every Christian.

Food For Thought

1. Call to mind your most intense experiences of loving and being loved. Do you agree that all loving is more alike than different? If not, why not?
2. Have you observed your relationships with others? Has evolution provided you with innate tendencies for altruism and forgiveness?
3. How do you resist love or fail to love? Is this the result of your early life? List strategies that you use to overcome your resistance to love.

Prayer

Invocation:
God, Our Loving Mother,
  Help us grow in love.
God, Our Loving Mother,
  Give us enduring love.
God, Our Loving Mother,
  Make our loves abundant.

Scripture: John 13:34–35

Response:
Let us pray for self-knowledge:

God Our Creator heal our wounds.
Let us pray for communion with others:
God Our Creator heal our wounds.
Let us pray for true deeds of love:
God Our Creator heal our wounds.

Prayer:

Christ, who opens the door of life to us, help us to enter into God's love. Dispel the fear and anxiety that slow our journey to you and your love. Make our hearts burn within us and let us recognize your presence. Let us be drawn to your light and joy and never turn back. Console us when we fail in love and grant us mercy and new hope. Amen.

Explore:

Listen to a favorite love song or read aloud a love poem that moves you. Write out the words and describe what moves you in the thoughts and feelings expressed. For instance, I am moved by sonnet 116 of Shakespeare for its understanding of love's commitment to communion and its power to withstand the challenge of time and difficulties. Then read the First Letter of John, chapter four, to see the way similar themes appear.

A similar exploration can be undertaken by considering a filmed love story or novel that you have responded to. What was it in the plot, characters or images that moved you and expanded or confirmed your view of love?

CHAPTER THREE

• MARRIAGE •

Marriage is surely one of the most complicated relationships that exists, and it gets more challenging all the time. As the standards for a good marriage increase it becomes harder to have one. It doesn't help that an unfriendly secular culture has little sympathy for fidelity and lifelong commitment. "Life's short, get a divorce," proclaimed a recent Chicago billboard erected by a firm of divorce lawyers. The ensuing public outcry forced the withdrawal of the lawyers' self-advertisement, but the message remains: If you are frustrated, disappointed and unhappy in your marriage, quit. A divorce culture urges you to leave while you're young enough to try again.

So-called "starter marriages" or "starter wives" are labels used in the media, while older rich men flaunt their second, third or fourth trophy wives. Celebrities change sexual partners with frequency, in between their marriages and divorces. Media coverage of these hook-ups and break-ups and marriage-go-rounds produce a cultural atmosphere that erodes commitment to promise keeping and fidelity.

Will marriage disappear? No, not very likely, but in a sexually permissive do-your-own-thing culture, the institution of faithful marriage has come under siege. Women often feel that they must struggle in order to stay permanently and happily married.

Millions of words are written analyzing the difficulties of women who want to wed, have children and pursue a career. Other books deplore the plight of older women who have been divorced, impoverished and abandoned to raise children alone. Often these treatments of marriage imply that things used to be better for women in the past. This nostalgia appears to be misplaced. I don't think that there has ever been a golden age of marriage from a woman's point of view.

The future may be better. Over the past centuries ideals of marriage in western culture have been evolving in a positive direction when it comes to women's equality. Theological Christian developments inspired secular ideals of universal human rights and equality that have been beneficial. The rights of man have been gradually extended to the rights of women, in civic and political life and in marriage. What has been called "the equal regard family" has become the ideal goal, a family in which the welfare of women, children and men are regarded as equal in worth. Male patriarchal power and privilege have given way in the west, at least in theory if not in practice.

Another huge influence on women's well being in marriage has been the advent of medical technology. In the United States, maternal and infant mortality has decreased and childbirth is safer. Children generally survive to adulthood. The medical control of maternal and infant death rates has been balanced by widespread control of fertility. Through knowledge and technologies of reproduction, married women can regulate their fertility; they can look forward to long healthy lives and to knowing their grown children and grandchildren.

Christian Teaching on Marriage

When taking an extended historical perspective, it can be said that Christian teachings on women and marriage *have* come a long way. Positive church perspectives on sex and marriage are the result of many factors, but one important development has been the growth of biblical scholarship. Today, mainline Christians no longer rely solely on fundamentalist or literal readings of texts. All Scripture must be interpreted in the church community. Why? Because while Scripture is inspired by the Holy Spirit it can have many different levels of meaning—moral and allegorical for instance—beyond the literal meaning of the words.

Scripture must always be interpreted and judged by the authoritative life, teachings and resurrection of Jesus Christ. Christ's words and deeds convey God's ultimate revelation. Every individual text is inspired by the Spirit and is also a human creation, and it must be seen as part of the whole of God's gospel.

Misogynist scriptural texts that denigrate women or command their silence or subordination to men now can be understood as products of a particular patriarchal cultural context that no longer should apply. Rather, the example and teaching of Christ essentially reveals women's equal dignity in the church, in the world and in marriage. Those Scriptures which proclaim God's impartiality and equal love of all the creation must be given decisive weight.

The foundational texts for women's equality in Christianity proclaim that "in Christ there is neither male nor female, slave or free, Jew or Greek, but all are one in Christ Jesus." Christian disciples are not judged by their gender but by their love of God and neighbor, the universal Christian vocation. The Holy Spirit blows where it will, and spiritual wisdom, vision and holiness are free gifts given to God's daughters and sons. Past church discriminations against women distorted the gospel good news of women's equality and worth. Pope John Paul II apologized to women for the past sins of the church and its members against them.

Yet women's rights were also recognized in early Christian practice in revolutionary ways that promised and then delivered progress for women over the centuries. From the beginning, women (along with slaves) flocked to Christianity because of the Christian affirmation of their moral equality. The value of women's role and service in the world is also affirmed by the Christian emphasis upon the works of mercy meeting the needs of the body and soul.

The human body is a temple of the Spirit for Christians and so the value of female bodies could not be reduced to the capacity for procreation and sexual pleasure. Christian women from the beginning could choose not to marry and live as dedicated virgins in the church community serving and worshiping God. Women, even slave women, were equally called to witness to Christ, and they too could become heroic martyrs for their faith.

As church law evolved over the centuries, women's equal rights in marriage were protected by the requirement that a woman must give her free consent to the marriage. These rules were developed with the concept of the marriage contract, and were often contested by powerful male heads of families who wished to marry off their women for dynastic or material advantages. Widows too had their rights protected to remain unmarried or to remarry. They were given dedicated roles in early Christian communities.

Another important Christian safeguard for women, expressed as early as in Augustine's time, prohibited men from putting away or divorcing infertile women. Failure to produce a male heir was no justification for divorce (the famous case of Henry VIII comes to mind), although exceptions were often made in practice. In general, however, the insistence on monogamy, or one wife for life, protected older women who were no longer fertile or sexually desirable.

Christian women were legally secure from being coerced into marriage, being discarded, divorced or losing their marital rights at the will of their husbands. Fidelity was enjoined equally upon both men and women and adultery prohibited for both. These early teachings on marriage and the developed canon laws were stepping stones to present modern teachings on the equality of men and women in Christian marriage.

Moreover, the early requirement for a freely consented mutual contract of marriage granted the right of each spouse to sexual access to the other. This obligation or duty became thought of as a debt to be paid. While wives could demand their sexual rights, the duty to obediently grant marital sexual rights fell more heavily upon women who might become pregnant. Today no more talk is found of a wife's duty to obediently submit to sex and pay the debt. Instead the free consent of a wife to sexual intercourse is morally granted, and coerced sex against a wife's will is recognized as marital rape.

Coercion and violence are no longer tolerated in marriage. Once widespread physical "chastisement"—wife-beating—is now judged to be morally abhorrent, a form of domestic abuse that is both sinful and illegal. Christians understand that love's equality and care is violated by any coercion in marriage. Domestic abuse is still widespread, but no longer socially acceptable in most of the Western world.

So too, "women's work" and activities outside the home—once deplored—are now seen as part of the Christian obligation to help create a civilization of love. In the church's social gospel, both men and women have equal responsibilities in the domestic, civic and public sphere to work for God's kingdom on earth.

The free mutual commitment of marriage creates a Christian family called to maintain and transform society. The family is recognized as the domestic church and must be given rights as the basic cell of every larger society.

Christian marriage is a sacrament because it mediates God's love to and through the union of the vowed pair. The sacrament of marriage, like other sacraments, is a visible sign of God's gracious gift of love. A sacramental marriage is created by the two persons who mutually promise themselves to each other; their mutual vow is the sacrament and the church serves as a witness to the bond. Church laws govern the practices of its members' sacramental marriages, while the laws of the secular state regulate the marriage rules of its citizens.

The essential core of the covenanted union of marriage is the mutually vowed gift of love, friendship, fidelity, sexual privilege and mutual support. Married love participates in Christ's loving self-gift to the world that engenders new life. As a Christian vocation, the marital union receives the Holy Spirit's assistance in fulfilling the commitment to love and serve one another. Where love and charity abide, there God is, where God is, love and joy are.

The fidelity and permanently willed promise of marriage imitates God's faithful covenant with humankind. As secular philosopher Hannah Arendt once expressed it, "a promise is a sacrament of the will." The will's commitment to love and be faithful is lived out in marriage just as God's steadfast love and good will is given to creation. The daring venture of Christian marriage is the willing promise to live and love no matter what the future brings.

New Thoughts and Challenges
Marriage is a permanent commitment, but when a relationship truly dies, must Christians remain single to receive the Eucharist? Certain circumstances allow for the church to issue a "declaration of nullity"—an annulment—but this process intimidates many divorced Catholics. Many prefer to ignore church teaching rather than investigate this option. Other Christian denominations tend to be more lax in their attitudes toward divorce and remarriage, making them attractive options for Catholics who wish to remarry. The issue is complicated and no one underestimates the hardship and heartbreak of a failed marriage. What we can all agree on is the need for more effective marriage preparation and better support for and ministry to married couples.

Another challenge to Christian marriage are the contrary views presented by other religious traditions, such as certain branches of Islam or fundamentalist sects that permit polygamy. One argument for polygamy is that the patriarchs in the Old Testament did it. Augustine explained away the polygamy of the patriarchs as a one-time exception made by God in order to build up the Jewish people. In populous Christendom, however, the faithful must adhere to God's original plan for marriage as put forth in Genesis and affirmed by Christ: a man and woman marry and become one flesh, a union which no man must put asunder.

Certainly, many contend that polygamy threatens the equality and rights of women. Monogamy's permanent marital commitment can more effectively safeguard the rights of women in marriage and in the larger society. In the practice of polygamy, women can be subject to insecurity from having to compete for their husband's favor, or having to struggle for their children's share of family resources. Multiple wives or mistresses threaten a wife's singular authority and dignity. If a wife is not submissive she can be demoted in status, or displaced in influence. In fact, the serial polygamy practiced in our modern divorce culture also works against the welfare of women and children.

Another debated marriage issue for Christians is the treatment of same-sex partners. Some Christian denominations have decided that in a marriage the two who become one may be a couple of the same gender. Those who disagree argue that only heterosexual marriage can exist; they cite Scripture and claim that the procreative purpose of marriage must be upheld. Even if in a heterosexual marriage the couple are infertile, or beyond the age of reproduction, they can maintain the procreative heterosexual form of the sexual act.

The official Catholic position prohibiting gay marriage arises from the present Vatican teaching that homosexuality is an objectively disordered condition and that same-sex sexual relations are always forbidden because they are neither procreative nor practiced within marriage. It is also asserted in papal teachings that men and women have been created with essentially different natures that are complementary. In a marriage a male and a female are needed to complete and complement each other in the union—which no same-sex marriage can do.

These understandings about gender and sex in marriage are the basis of church teachings that each conjugal act must be open to procreation. Artificial contraception and sterilization are forbidden and, of course, the church condemns abortion in all circumstances.

Despite this consistent teaching on these controversial issues, it is no secret that there is a great deal of dissent and unrest over many of the church's positions on sex, gender and marriage. Yet it is also fair to say that today, as compared to all of history and to other cultural conditions, there is greater potential for Christian marriages to fulfill the highest of Christian ideals of love and equality.

Stages and Varieties of Marriage

One perpetual difficulty in speaking in general about marriage is that each marriage is particular, and indeed unique. Marriages are as different in kind as the people involved. The variety of marriages that exist and last can also go through different stages over the years. A long-married woman can report that she has had at least six marriages—all to the same man.

There is the young beginner's marriage in which the partners must grow up together and adjust to (the shock of?) adult responsibility. As a young wife I could not believe how much I had taken for granted in my parents' household—for years and years someone else had been buying the groceries, paying the bills and cleaning the toilet and bathroom floor.

When babies first arrive, a revolutionary stage of marriage begins, one in which the vital needs of little people are overwhelming and have to be met every minute of the day and night, with no time off. Young parents become comrades in arms in fighting the good fight.

As the children survive and begin to grow up, an extended pre-middle-aged marriage emerges which is also fully (and frantically?) engaged in intensive family and career building. Things may only begin to calm down for a married pair as young adult offspring are launched. Then a more focused marriage—along with semi-retirement—may begin. This gradually and slowly evolves into an old marriage that has to face the inevitable endgame and finale.

In satisfying, long-lasting marriages where reasonably healthy partners enjoy fairly fortunate circumstances, the later years can be rewarding. One man mused that his marriage was "like a long complicated meal, with the last years consisting of dessert." Well maybe, but a more apt description might be that later marriage is like the final movement of a long symphony in which different themes and variations are being brought into a harmonious and satisfying resolution. In fruitful final movements of a marital symphony, the partners can finally arrive at a stage when they have more leisure to enjoy each other, enjoy their families and visit their friends—at least those friends who are still alive and well enough to welcome visits.

After a certain age old friends and relatives begin to die off or become subject to the plagues of disease, disability and dementia. "Come south and visit me while I can still remember who you are," warns an Alabama cousin. Grandchildren too must be visited speedily and often, first to know who they are and secondly because they grow up in a flash and are off to college.

Those marriages that manage to finish up strong benefit from the sheer accumulation of experience from many years spent together. So much shared happiness, sorrow, conflict and resolution can produce a magnetic binding force that energizes a couple. It becomes virtually impossible not to be or stay married "until death do you part"—which is not so far away anymore. As always the approach of death clarifies the mind wonderfully.

A sense of gratitude wells up over the fact that you both are still alive, sill conscious, still functioning and still able to love and take care of one another. Now that we know that altruism is rewarding in itself and an evolved innate human predisposition, we can understand how many older married people keep on nurturing their spouse through thick and thin. You see older married couples helping each other in the grocery store, in the doctor's office, in every emergency room and nursing facility. It is a consoling truth that loving and caring are innate and increase in strength through practice.

It turns out from other psychological studies that humans love the familiar—just as much as they delight in the novel. The familiarity of an aging spouse's face elicits affection. Even the aging body of a mate can evoke fondness, if for nothing else, the grateful memory of many past pleasures and work projects achieved together. "Thanks for the memories," Bob Hope used to sing as he signed off his radio show.

As for those more awful memories of mutual damage and injury inflicted in a marriage, they can lose their force as they recede into a crowded past. The ability to forgive fully becomes easier over time. Forgiveness, cooperation and peacemaking are other positive capacities that evolutionary psychologists now think developed in order to aid group survival. Surely these traits become virtues that are fostered by religion and moral ideals. The tolerance and serenity often displayed by older people can be genuine and not just a matter of fatigue.

Since marriages differ in how much mutual or unilateral harm has been inflicted in the past and how much has been resolved the amount of mutual harmony between spouses may also vary. Certain exemplary divorced persons are even able to forgive their ex-mates.

The clashing unfinished marital symphony or crashed roller coaster ride can be survived and remembered benevolently rather than angrily. All the still-married persons also have to overcome that attractive innate human tendency, the desire for vindication and thirst for revenge. Bitterness takes a high psychic toll; in the remains of the day as Shakespeare writes, "ripeness is all."

Varieties of Marriage
Unbelievably there do seem to be marriages that are made in heaven and have little experience of the petty depths to which vicious marital conflicts can descend. In a completely compatible home sweet home there's never been heard a discouraging word and the skies are sunny all day. Two spouses can be so similarly easygoing or so positively complementary that they agree on all matters large or small, or agree to disagree.

Stable, peaceful marriages are often between couples who come from the same cultural, ethnic and religious background; they may have married the boy or girl next door, or their older brother's or sister's best friend. All their implicit assumptions about life are alike and provide bedrock for the marital solidity. Moreover, marriages made in heaven often share a common religious belief about the best way to heaven.

A WOMAN'S PERSPECTIVE

Two married Christians who keep the faith and worship and pray together are blessed in the resources they possess to keep loving and working together.

Other marital pairs will start out with very different backgrounds, personal beliefs and temperamental affinities and they never get more alike or more compatible. These marriages that survive their unfavorable odds usually have surmounted much internal turbulence. Celebrating their golden anniversary is a high achievement. They stayed the course and at least lived out a commitment to promise keeping.

But no matter how difficult or easy going, every marriage will have to confront its own unique array of the slings and arrows of outrageous fortune. Even middle class Americans living in an era of peace and prosperity can still encounter natural disasters, chance accidents and necessary losses stemming from disease and the deaths of loved ones. Each blow takes its toll and requires resilience.

In the end, long-married spouses, whatever their journey, can be grateful for having completed their long distance race. But the image of a race, or that of a symphony, may not do justice to the dramas of married and family life. Marriage is more like being on a roller coaster ride at the amusement park, or starring in a long-running soap opera with many twists and turns to the plot. If there is no derailment or cancellation of the drama, survival produces exhilaration.

To take a political analogy for the achievement of marital union, the process can be likened to the struggle that took place at the constitutional convention in Philadelphia. To form a more perfect union, two sovereign persons cannot avoid patiently hammering out compromises. In marriage a couple must agree on a common rule for their practice of religion, morality, sex, childbearing, work, finance, food, friendship, leisure and aesthetic taste. Decorating a home together can be as trying a test of compromise as any other.

Two different temperaments, sets of values, tastes, work preferences and emotional styles of play have to be knitted together. Two personal stories, each starring "me, myself and I," must be melded into a new and larger narrative, with new supporting casts of friends, colleagues and kin.

To make marriage all the more complicated a venture, each individual partner is constantly changing and growing. In each personality many different levels of consciousness are operating simultaneously in tandem with the ongoing relationship and joint marriage project. Invisible interpersonal and emotional dynamics operate in a common marital life.

While persons can love one another and be sincerely committed, they may yet experience obscure eruptions of negative and selfish feelings. No one is fully healed of childhood wounds or character weaknesses. Cold fronts and obscure changes in the emotional weather map occur constantly in marriages (except for those marriages made in heaven!). Outbursts of anger or frustration or depression can darken the atmosphere.

Happily, however, the sun also rises and breaks through the gloom. Mysterious upsurges of love, erotic attraction, humor and affection can disperse the clouds and enliven the day. Emotional highs and peaceful moments of contentment arrive and recede in the changing environment of the marital landscape.

Not only is every marriage unique and different in its path, but a marriage can also be experienced differently by the partners. The claim has been made, for example, that the wife's marriage differs from that of the husband's. Can this always be true?

The inability of outsiders to know the hidden inside story of other marriages is legendary. Why in the world did she marry him, or how can he stand to live with her? Or, why is such a perfect couple getting a divorce? Perhaps the mystery can be partly explained by the fact that even a married pair may be at sea about their voyage from time to time.

Do you always know it if you are happily married? Perhaps a satisfying marriage, or functioning marriage is as happy as a marriage can be.

And surely it makes a difference at what point in time an assessment is being made or the marital temperature is taken; a white hot quarrel can produce rage and resentment, with a longing for divorce or, better yet, widowhood, that may retroactively color the past. Everyone has known of post-divorce shifts in attitudes toward an ex-mate. All memory is constructed in the present and is affected by a person's current mood and circumstances.

Certainly, the children in a family can each have their own version of their parents' marriage. This may not be surprising since each child comes into a different family configuration—which will be further changed by their entrance. Parents as spouses are playing different roles in the ongoing family drama, responding to each other, reacting to their children who are in turn reacting to them and to siblings.

Realistically too, shifts of power and marital influence appear when income, health, habits, sex appeal and careers flourish or fade. While it shouldn't be so, women who earn an income equal to or more than their husbands often feel more freedom in making family decisions. Husbands may feel threatened by a wife's success at work or at home.

Overcoming subtle forms of marital and parental competition can be a challenge for imperfect, insecure human beings. In two-career modern marriages insidious questions can intrude. Is your career more successful, or more morally worthwhile than mine? Do you have more friends and social success, and whom do the children love best? Human egoism may never be thoroughly banished.

More destructively, a spouse succumbing to drink or drugs also changes and distorts the dynamics of a marriage. So too does an affair, a serious illness, a traumatic accident or economic collapse. Many marriages founder and do not weather crises and tragedies. A child's death or serious mental impairment like autism is known to be correlated with divorce.

Marital breakdowns and divorces demoralize other married people, because marriages exist as small oases of love and mutual support in the indifferent desert. When a marriage falls apart, a basic cell of civilization dies and the disintegration dims the hope for survival of others seeking stability. Epidemics of divorce, no-fault or otherwise, subtly weaken the culture's institution of marriage.

Everyone has at one time or another held their breath while their married friends and relatives go through troubles. An apt metaphor of marital conflict and survival is the biblical story of Jacob wrestling through the night with the mysterious stranger/angel. Despite suffering a wounded hip, Jacob will not let go until he receives his opponent's blessing. Only with daybreak does the blessing arrive. The moral is clear: If you don't let go or give in, morning can come at last with its returning light. Couples may limp into their future with only minor wounds which may eventually heal.

Persons live forward in time and the present moment is always open to the unpredictable event. Hopes for fruitful marriages persist because human beings can learn, change and grow in love and wisdom. Realistically, friends, families, parishes and communities can offer support to marriages along the way.

Church programs, such as marriage encounter, may offer help. Psychotherapy and marriage counseling also provide tools and opportunities for growing up and together. "Can this marriage be saved?" is a riveting title of a regular women's magazine feature that has been running for years.

Blessedly, despite stormy seas, many marriages sail into homeport. These marriages can serve as mainstays and inspiration for others. Good marriages that last almost always diffuse goodness. They provide hospitality, encouragement, good counsel and other works of mercy. Yet each of these lasting unions is unique and follows no detailed blueprints. Happy families are not all alike, but differ each in their own way.

Spiritual Challenges in Marriage

In fruitful marital love, a union is achieved while individuals flourish and increase in their unique development. The Christian ideal of loving union is not one of complete fusion and loss of self identity. Nor should one person in the marriage dominate, absorb or incorporate the other. Neither can it be claimed that well-married people have simply contracted a successful business partnership of two autonomous associates.

Actually, the giving and receiving in a loving intersubjective union creates a dynamic new whole that is larger than the sum of its parts and possesses synergy. However, the parts remain distinct and are even strengthened in their individuality—I learn from you and become changed, but I also see how we are separate and distinct.

Love, as we have described it in earlier chapters, can create a mutual consciousness that simultaneously increases the shared bond and the individual at the same time. As individuals move beyond themselves to unite with the other in love they receive love in return. In empathy lovers can feel with the other and take the role of the other, expanding the heart and the mind.

Love is God's win-win game in which the more you give the more you receive. The new creative whole that is engendered gives birth to surprises in married life. Milton wrote that the chief end of marriage is "a meet and fitting conversation," and the "meet," or good back and forth of the dialogue produces a new story played out on many levels.

The greatest motivating force of human beings is the desire to love and be loved and to know and be known. Intimacy, love and friendship are the great human goods that we seek. A committed marriage gives partners the time, space and the inspiration to find the heart's desire. Can any other circumstance of life be so effective in forcing you to grow up and learn to love—over and over?

Marriage creates a relationship to which two persons bring their weaknesses and unhealed wounds from the past. The challenge to grow up and learn to love is always a part of Christian life, only more so in marriage. The greatest stumbling blocks to spiritual progress are selfishness, pride, self-ignorance and defensive self-deception that mar relationships with others.

CREATING NEW LIFE, NURTURING FAMILIES

In the intimacy of a modern marital commitment, there's no lasting hiding place or chance for disguise. Here you get to see yourself as another does. Earlier traditional marriage following conventional rules set down by custom may have not demanded so much personal intimacy or so many stark confrontations. A psychological unity of equal and open friendship was not expected.

Men may have only had other men as friends and women remained at home in female circles of relatives and neighbors. The book titled *Down Among the Women and Children* described the usual social structure.

As men and women's education and roles in life become more equal and similar, their union can be richer and deeper. More conflicts may ensue, but more rewards will come from resolving them. More spiritual growth comes from the challenges offered in an equal friendship.

Married persons confront each other as peers and equals; they can admonish each other and inspire one another to be their best selves. They are shaping each other up in a process of mutual maturation that in an earlier day we called "mutual sanctification." Managing the dance or negotiating and working through the necessary compromises takes energy, constant dialogue and wisdom.

Spouses see you at your worst moments but they also see and appreciate those fine hidden gestures that no one else may ever see. Tenderness and courtesy can be quietly offered and received in private. Sexual love is one deep hidden part of the marital iceberg that is not public—at least in affluent households with separate bedrooms. A shared sense of humor may be another binding force that is not always on view. Wit is spontaneous and a playful merry spirit goes a long way in the grim grown-up world.

A good marriage transforms persons in a plethora of ways. Empathy, attentiveness and caregiving increase love in its embodied face to face mode. Marital communication can become incredibly subtle because one knows the other and is intimately known. Of course this intimacy that feeds love also makes it possible to hurt each other deeply. There is no conflict as potentially lethal as marital conflict.

One of the most important characteristics that a marriage must develop is the ability to resolve conflicts forthrightly and fairly. Many married people come from conflict avoidance cultures and families and they have a hard time learning to formulate their difficulty or mastering the art of voicing a problem. Tolerating dissension or disagreement is difficult for many religious persons with their ideals of love. The fact that there will be inevitable conflicts of interest between the best of friends and lovers is both a disappointment and a challenge.

Other more assertive, feisty partners have grown up in families and milieus which have no problem with expressing criticism or grievances. For them the marital challenge lies in curbing engrained habits of irritability, critique, opposition and angry confrontations. In matters of conflict, disagreement and differences, Christian couples have to master the middle way. They must not always suppress their feelings but also employ the self-control of tongue and actions.

The art of amicable disagreement and dialogue is a delicate one. The emergence of assertiveness training programs reveals the cultural deficit among many nice Americans. Other therapeutic efforts also can help people to see themselves plain as well as learn to avoid being overcome by emotional wildfires or emotional flooding. The tried and true ideal in Christian spiritual formation is particularly important for marriage, i.e., that disciples who grow up in Christ will become free enough to control their thoughts, emotions and actions in the practice of love of neighbor.

Christians can be helped to live up to their own ideals by psychotherapies and self-help groups, but they also can draw upon rich religious resources for personal transformation: Prayer, worship, Scripture reading, meditation, examination of conscience, confession and seeking counsel and inspiration in the lives of the saints—living and dead. The church offers food for the spiritual journey.

Love's humility, gentleness and generosity encourage habits of listening to others without hostility or insecure demands for control. Kindness and patience are the antidotes to contempt, the attitude known as the most lethal marriage slayer. In research and videos of married couples in counseling, those who displayed contempt for one another were at the highest risk of divorce.

This finding of marital research should come as no surprise to those disciples who take seriously Jesus' words on the danger of hellfire for those who call another a fool. Contempt and disgust are emotions that are the opposite of humility and love because they annihilate and discount another's humanity. Empathetic taking the role of the other is the very opposite of cutting, contemptuous sarcasm.

When married Christians morally fail in love, or commit a sin, then the Christian commandment to confess and seek forgiveness helps marital reconciliation. Married people can strive to abide by Paul's admonition to never let the sun set on their anger. But they also can take preventive measures against anger by meditating on Paul's scriptural descriptions of love's characteristics, as described in the previous chapter.

Christians who have been taught to examine their conscience and follow its dictates can further reconciliation after failures by confessing, making restitution and forgiving one another. There is no need to try to forget the past, but injuries that have been forgiven tend to recede from awareness and lose their sting. Forgiveness is the food and fuel of the marriage commitment. The assistance of the Holy Spirit can be counted upon to move mind and heart toward married love and fruitfulness.

Marriage produces many goods and fruits that are obvious to objective researchers. Everything from health to wealth to happiness is reported to be higher among the married. Creating and sustaining households through cooperative work, having and raising children, investing in communities—all of these are goods. But the personal spiritual journey of a marriage also produces fruits.

Fruits of Marriage

A fruit of the Spirit is joy. Those who seek God's love through marriage will find joy as well. Delight in the presence of the beloved quickens the commitment to marriage. The vowed promise may sustain one through hard times, but the joy and happiness of being merrily accompanied makes fidelity easy. This yoke is light.

Unique marriages have different styles of flourishing. The love of peace and domestic tranquility can give a quiet happiness to the less adventurous, but those with more restless temperaments may need higher seas to nourish them in familial fidelities. *Semper fi* works for the Marine Corps because it accompanies vigorous activity and challenge, and the same holds true for some adventurous spouses.

But whatever level of activity, change or achievements a lasting marriage produces, the spouses can know the happiness of a good and virtuous life. Commitment, fidelity and chastity become natural and energizing. Long-married people can grow to look like one another because they have mirrored each other in face to face empathy for so long. Instead of being bent out of shape, married partners become bent into shape, welded together. They are engrafted, and woven together in a web with a thousand linked threads.

The supportive web of an extended consciousness enhances individuality and liveliness. The play and interplay of marital conversation spurs breadth and vitality. Even some benign competition can give sparkle to the emotional marital landscape. The discipline and focus required of commitment gives individual personality more acuity and depth.

The long struggle to leave intractable human narcissism behind ends in a liberating freedom to take oneself lightly. Humor and laughter is essential for a good married life because laughter erupts when unexpected upsets of order occur and marriage is full of surprises. Comic ups and downs mark married life.

Humor, wit, laughter and elaborate forms of play bring light and gaiety to equal marriages between friends who give love to one another.

God loves the cheerful giver according to the Scriptures, and when God rests you merry, then the heart burns with enduring warmth.

Two can always be merrier than one. Joy and laughter are infectious and the opposite of grudging and resentful gloominess and proud isolation. Like laughter, erotic romantic love occurs always and everywhere in humankind.

Love and desire impel individuals to live together as one. "Come live with me and be my love." Marriage, or a bonded pair, is the most ancient and human practice; it creates humankind by giving birth to new individuals and sustaining group life.

In the time before Vatican II, marriage was described in the nuptial mass as "the greatest happiness known to man in this vale of tears." I remember smiling over this "sentimentality," but now I know better. Alas, the vale of tears will be part of every life journey and a good marriage is the staff and rod that gets you through alive and in one piece. At joyful anniversaries of long-married and grateful persons it is fitting to meditate on the promising lines from Psalm 92:

> The righteous flourish like the palm tree,
>   and grow like a cedar in Lebanon.
> They are planted in the house of the LORD;
>   they flourish in the courts of our God.
> In old age they still produce fruit;
>   they are always green and full of sap,
> showing that the LORD is upright;
>   he is my rock and there is no unrighteousness in him.
> (Psalm 92:12–15)

FOOD FOR THOUGHT

1. What is your understanding of Christian marriage? Have your views of marriage changed from those you received in youth? How?
2. What forces have you experienced working against Christian marriage in the world, and what resources have helped you to cope and flourish?

3. How have you grown up and become more loving over the years of being married? Give examples of ways that your individuality has increased through building a unique common life. Reflect on marital conflicts that have been resolved and observe any repeated patterns in the marriage relationship.

4. Every reader will also have had first hand experience of dozens of marriages in her circle of friends and family. Reflect on the good marriages you have encountered and what they seem to have in common despite their uniqueness. Then think of the failing or broken marriages you have known and note the harmful attitudes and practices that were destructive.

PRAYER

Invocation:
God of Love and Truth,
  Replenish our hearts daily.
God of Love and Truth,
  Give care to my speech.
God of Love and Truth,
  Give me a willing spirit.

Scripture: 1 Corinthians 13:4–7

Response:
Let us pray that we grow and learn to love more fully:
  Help us to be patient and kind.
Let us pray that we can see ourselves as God sees us:
  Help us to be humble and merry.
Let us pray to become steadfast and true-hearted:
  Help us to keep our promises in all things.

Prayer:

Loving God we desire to love our spouse and grow up into Christ's holy kindness and patience. Help us overcome all the immature selfishness that we bring to married loving. Enable us to bring to birth a union that helps us flourish together and as individuals. Grant us grateful hearts to praise and rejoice in the gift of marriage. Amen.

CHAPTER FOUR

• SEXUALITY •

Women who marry embrace sexual love as a way to God. When Christians affirm that "Whatever you do, in word or work do for the glory of God," (Colossians 3:17), sex is included. But until the modern era little attention was paid to a spirituality of marital sexuality. A religious or spiritual vocation referred to vowed celibacy and sexual abstinence. An active sexual life of holiness could hardly be envisioned. Why not?

Obstacles

Historically, sexual abstinence and offering up one's sexuality to God was assumed to be the better and more perfect way to holiness—even in the married state. Husbands and wives were more holy the more they imitated vowed religious celibates and abstained from sex. Many traditional accounts of saintly married partners praise the way that the couple gave up their sexual relations altogether, sometimes after having procreated children, but sometimes from the beginning. Abstinent spouses might eventually go their separate ways to join or found new religious communities. Widows and widowers with their active sexual and reproductive life safely over, could also have an inside track to the short list of canonized married persons.

Such negative attitudes to sexual activity lingered on into the present era. So-called "white marriages" without sexual expression have been piously practiced and other "brother-sister marriages" were recommended for legally married couples finding themselves in canonically invalid unions. Other married persons who could not risk having more children for some valid reason such as health, could also be advised to practice sexual abstinence for the rest of their fertile years. With the advent of old age, as Augustine noted, it would be easier to live the celibate ideal in the married state. He, however, was troubled by the shaming fact that he experienced sexual dreams and temptations to the end of his life.

At the same time that Augustine and other theologians of his time upheld the superiority of celibacy, they always remained careful to defend and recognize the goods of marriage—the procreation of children, the vowed faithful union of the partners and marital friendship with its mutual support. Sexual intercourse aimed at the generation of children would be considered a good, even though it included the danger of sexual pleasure. Marital sex also guarded against lust, fornication and illicit sexuality, as in the famous phrase, "better to marry than burn." In later formulations, sexual intercourse was seen as a contractual right, or debt to be paid by each spouse to the other.

In the midst of this somewhat ambivalent tradition toward actual marital sexuality in marriages, the nuptial and wedding imagery of Scripture was enthusiastically embraced as a Christian symbol of fulfilled love. Building on imagery from the Hebrew Scriptures—The Song of Songs is replete with bridal and sexual imagery—the church used gospel metaphors such as the "marriage of the lamb," and spoke of Christ as the "bridegroom" of the church. Old Testament nuptial images of God as the husband of unfaithful Israel also appeared. But descriptions of the sexual joy, union and delight of marriage were minimized or absent. The marital and wedding imagery focused upon the feasting and joy of the celebration rather than sexual pleasure or union. In the tradition the very erotic sexuality of the Song of Songs was spiritualized and interpreted as referring to the soul's love of God.

Unfortunately, in the time of the early church a tainted and negative view of the body and sex seeped into Christian thought. A dualistic model of human nature became dominant, influenced by Greek and

Platonic thought. Man was seen as a two-fold organism with a lower animal material body joined to a higher rational immaterial soul. The higher imperishable soul was destined to return to eternal life while the vulnerable material body was doomed to decay and death. The soul could only be completely fulfilled and free after it "shuffled off its mortal coil." Bodily functioning was unclean and shameful because it was animalistic, carnal and dying. The material body was irrational, lethal and corrupting and so must be controlled and overcome by penance and self-denial.

In this severely dualistic and rationalistic picture of human nature the sexual drive held the greatest dangers for the mind and soul's control or abstinence. The innate animal sexual desire was known as powerful, pervasive and involuntary. The intensity of sexual pleasure meant that it was hard to control and discipline. Sexual pleasure must be detached through the rational soul's domination. Involuntary physical and emotional responses should be governed or avoided through reason and the acquisition of virtue.

Overwhelming emotions or passions were thought to originate from the threatening, despised animal nature. Strong emotions, especially sexual desire could overcome rational self-control. No man in the thrall of sexual passion could hope to engage in philosophical deliberation or meditative contemplation. Sex was an obstacle to virtue. Sex was also held to be unhealthy by some ancient physicians. Men were considered to lose vital energies along with their sperm, and of course women (in actual fact) faced injury and death from the complications of childbirth. Dedicated virginity and male vocations of celibacy avoided the moral and physical dangers involved in sexuality.

Early Christian moralists also could see the sexual abuses and exploitative practices in the pagan cultures that surrounded them. Unbridled lust for pleasure resulted in widespread promiscuity and with the inequality of power in a hierarchical slave society, the poor and the vulnerable, particularly women, were abused. Rape was common, in and out of warfare, and slaves of both genders were sexually exploited at the will of their masters. Women, even higher class women, were considered inferior to men and were utilized for procreating offspring and obtaining sexual pleasure. Women were often involuntarily married off to much older men to ensure the family lineage or material advantages.

When the body, emotions and sexuality are despised as animalistic and exploited for their utility, women will be denigrated and suffer grievously. Women's bodies are so clearly sexual, reproductive and carnal. When bodily emissions are thought to be polluting and unclean, women who are constantly bleeding, giving birth and nursing will be constantly unclean. Not only are fleshly women's bodies polluting but they are objects of sexual desire and temptation. They must be segregated and controlled. When ideals of vowed celibacy operated within male dominated, flesh-despising culture, then women became dangerous and despised. Blatant misogyny pervaded ancient cultures and succeeded in infiltrating Christian religious thought.

In such circumstances of inequality and prejudice against women and sexuality, it is hard to imagine sexual intercourse as an expression of mutual love or that sexual pleasure can possess an intrinsic goodness. When women are not free moral and sexual agents, it is hard to integrate active sexual pleasure into moral and religious development. Virtue could be seen to lie in either celibacy or in strictures against illicit adultery or fornication and in obligations to procreate, and integrating sexual pleasure into a virtuous marital life would be difficult. Penitential abstinence and moderation in marriage could be approved but not a celebration of love's passion and pleasure. Fasting yes, feasting no.

Deep prejudices against the body, against sexuality and against women are linked and prove hard to eradicate. They can linger on in different forms into the present. Many developing children can be infected with bodily shame as they are socialized into control of their bodily functions. Disgust with the lack of bodily control can be conveyed by puritanical families. The punitive forbidding of childhood erotic pleasures can produce anxious sexual fears and shame over being embodied and vulnerable. Fears, anxieties and sexual shame can be explicitly or implicitly conveyed to children.

Our present hyper-sexualized culture and media have their own ways of distorting sexual development. As in the ancient world, sinful sexual corruptions of lust, pornography, rape, sexual abuse and sexual trafficking of women and children are still features of western society. Abortion and sexual diseases are rampant. Children must be warned against sexual diseases and sexual abuse in their own communities. Overt sexual abuse is devastating and produces long lasting consequences.

Women are still subject to sexual coercion and sexual aggression in and out of marriages. Socially approved widespread promiscuity among young persons trivializes sexuality and produces developmental distortions. The hook-up culture works against romantic love, courtship and faithful marital commitment. Women in particular suffer from a society that exploits them and their bodies in the name of sexual freedom. They can end up feeling conflicted over the commercial exploitation of the female body and female sexuality. Negative cultural attitudes toward sexuality can cloud a woman's sexual development. Christian women may have to struggle to develop a positive and joyful sense of sexual maturity and virtue. How can it be done?

Welcome Changes
Beginning with Vatican II, church teaching on sex and marriage blossomed. Sexual love as an expression of personal union engendering intimacy and friendship was valued. The end of loving union has been seen as an equal goal in marriage; sexuality is valued for its uniting power as well as for engendering children. Children may or may not be conceived, and children grow up and leave home, while marital sexual unity and love can last for life. Indeed, it is now understood that the loving bond of parents is all important in rearing the children that are conceived and born. Continuing sexuality between a mated pair has

been an evolutionary development because it serves the permanent bonding of two parents whose caretaking serves the survival and flourishing of children. Sexual union grounds marriages and kinship in families which are the base of human society and civilization.

Today the goodness of the body and sexual pleasure are affirmed to be God's great and good gift to humankind. The late Pope John Paul II wrote extensively on the theology of the body and celebrated the goodness of marital love and pleasure. He also made efforts to canonize more married saints.

Christians today understand that married people should strive to be holy *through, with* and *in* their sexual life together. A mutually loving embodied self-giving in marriage ideally encompasses both erotic passion and charity. The vowed commitment of marital union is fittingly consummated by sexual intercourse as the couple become "one flesh." Best of all, theologians now assert that each act of intercourse, whether potentially procreative or not, concretely reenacts the loving vowed gift of mutual commitment. Each sexual act throughout the marriage is linked to the initial and continuing vow, reenacting unity in the present moment. Fulfilling the past promise in the present gives assurance for the future.

The marital bond is strengthened by repeated experiences of love, pleasure and joy. Love grows strong through practiced expressions embodying sexuality, because one's body has its own nonverbal language of gift. Sexual acts can be recognized as an embodied form of communication that is as potent as the spoken word. Like a language there is a grammar of appropriate expression and an ethic of use: We must say what we mean and mean what we say both sexually and linguistically. Fidelity to love and to the partner is essential as is true speech.

The sexual union of loving couples is a form of praise and is intrinsically good in itself. When Saint Thomas taught that the pleasure of a good act is morally good, then marital sexual pleasure can be known as good and not as merely a concession to the need for release or to fulfill the goal of procreation. Of course, as with all human acts, prudence and tact must ensure that sexual encounters take place with loving courtesy—in the appropriate time and with the right mutual intention. But once the waters are known to be clear then diving headlong and playfully into erotic depths is good. Even splashing around in the shallows produces gladness and delight. In fact, the full range of a couple's life together can be expressed sexuality—from joyful peaks of passion to consoling comfort.

What most distressed an earlier rational view of sexuality is now considered as an essential part of God's gracious gift. The involuntary spontaneous quality of desire and sexual pleasure is what refreshes human life. Desire liberates the mind from its incessant rational deliberation and efforts to defensively control events. A lover can surrender to the cascading flow of passion and become enhanced by transcendent transporting delight. Sexual pleasure and joy enlarges and lifts the heart in the same way that beauty, art, music, nature and laughter are life giving. Critics have lied when they described orgasm as "a little death" or asserted that "all animals are sad after sex." No, passionate love should be recognized as a little birth that brings peace and companionable happiness. A new song has been sung in harmony and synchrony.

When desire increases and is fulfilled a wonderful insight appears over what it means to want something and what it is to get it. This is the ultimate win-win game, for the more I desire the more I incite ardor and desire and vice versa. The more I give the more I receive and all as effortless gratuitous gift. The embodied and ardent action of loving and desiring takes away all squeamishness or residual shame of the body's vulnerability. To love another's body fully in intercourse prepares us to love and appreciate other human bodies in whatever their stages and conditions. The intensity of the present moment in sexual loving is healing as it draws upon the deep wells of being in creation. Ardent attention is focused intensely in the moment and the old spiritual maxim of "do what you are doing" applies.

When ecstatic mutual pleasures are received then thoughts too can take flight. When Christ tells his disciples to lose the self in order to find it he is describing a natural and spiritual transcendent process in which the measure you give is the measure you receive. Many ecstatic prayers have soared to the heavens in praise and gratitude for the pleasure of sexual union. This joy, which expresses and creates love and then seeks more love and joy, may give some hint of the way that God loves creation. Embodied sexual ecstasy might also be a foretaste of the resurrected body. Perhaps a resurrected human body enjoys such happy plenitude of individual joy while in union with others. Individuality and communion are simultaneously enhanced in sexual joy.

The Challenge and Fruits of Sexual Love

All of the fruits of the Spirit— love, joy, gentleness, kindness, humility, patience and self control—will nurture sexual passion in marriage. A mutual sexual relationship must be developed together and is enhanced by the maturity and goodness of the partners. Sexual loving is partly an art which becomes more excellent with practice, but the caring unselfish character of the lovers remains most important. Sensitive lovers are intimately attentive and attuned to one another, just as a mother is attentive and responsive in affirming her child. Sexual loving affirms the embodied self that blooms with the self-confidence that happiness brings.

Knowing and being known in an enduring sexual union also works to further transparency, honesty and truthfulness. Committed sexual loving can give each partner a safe haven where personal vulnerabilities, rejections and wounds can be healed through love's mutual assurance and comforting delight. The burdens of life can be lightened by sexual love's rest and respite. Positive emotions, such as love and joy, are now psychologically recognized to have powers to heal and undo hurt and injuries. As explained in earlier chapters, emotions get their communicative powers from innate mirror systems in the brain that imitate and mirror another's responses. Empathy is an innate capacity and operates to make emotions contagious.

As humans we can share interpersonal consciousness and bond intensely with those we love. Brains, minds, bodies and emotions can become synchronized and united. Love enhances empathy and conveys affirmation to another through gestures, movements, touch and shared pleasure. Loving union can be transforming. In difficult circumstances married sexual union can strengthen and sustain a couple's struggles against adversity. Internal conflicts in a marriage can also be healed by sexual union, which affirms the fundamental love and commitment of a married pair.

In an imperfect world filled with flawed human beings, the challenging married relationship will always face difficulties of adjustment and conflicts of interest. Sexual union can engender forgiveness through nonverbal communication and through the present moment's capacity to create new beginnings. People make love to make love increase. Sex can be a bridge over troubled waters building and uniting love.

Humans are such body/mind/spirit unities that positive behavioral actions can generate new feelings. Initiating a loving gesture can release a feeling of love. Or as the maxim truthfully asserts, "Move a muscle, change a thought." Of course it is even more obvious that changing a thought can change an emotion or initiate an action. Mature human beings have many voluntary options through which to exercise their freedom and initiative.

Intentional human actions open the way to involuntary responses. At times the involuntary sexual responses of the bodily self have to be courted by voluntary actions. A dancer must diligently begin voluntarily moving through space before being carried away into following the music. Good sexual wooing is an art because it takes practice and knowledge of the process, of the self and of the other. Sexual desire is a gift, but it can be opened by focused attention and directed gestures. In stressed, overworked and fatigued modern marriages it can be difficult to obtain the time to cultivate loving sexual engagement.

Work can consume and exhaust spouses. Children's needs clamor to be met. Interruptions and distractions intrude on leisure time and make satisfying sexual unions difficult. And as in any starvation process, deprivation can begin to extinguish hunger, or in this case, sexual desire. Enkindling sexual joy and playfulness requires leisure. Even the emphasis upon achieving goals and controlling the body can be counterproductive. In married life it can be crucial to see loving sexual relations as important as keeping the Sabbath celebration.

An intimate sexual union is sensitive to every variation of personal and social change. In our self-help information culture we can be made aware of physical and emotional impairments that may be helped by therapeutic interventions. Even in the best of long enduring marriages there can arise illnesses, physical separations and other negative factors working against sexual union. Fatigue and diminishments of energy in old age may be unavoidable. Human beings live "at the will of the body" in many ways and health and sexual activity are not fully under our control.

But married lovers can run as good a race as can be run. They have set out to be married and married they will be. Love can endure and flourish despite difficulties. In the endgame of life a couple's long practice of sexual loving may sustain the loving tenderness needed for mutual caretaking. While memory lasts, gratitude wells up for those God given gifts of sexual pleasure and joy we have received.

With my body I thee wed.

Food for Thought

1. Write an informal sexual autobiography reflecting upon your earliest experiences and attitudes toward sex. What understandings and misunderstandings did you have as a child and young girl? Describe your

family's attitudes (explicit and implicit) toward sexuality that they conveyed to you.
2. Reflect on your personal and sexual development as a woman. Were there positive Christian influences in your journey or negative ones?
3. Have you grown emotionally and morally through your sexual experiences of giving and receiving love and pleasure? How?

Prayer

Invocation:
God Our Creator,
   Enliven our bodily being.
God Our Creator,
   Increase our sexual energy and joy.
God Our Creator,
   Enkindle our passionate love for our spouse.

Scripture: Song of Solomon 8:6–7

Response:
Let us pray for the power to give ourselves in sexual generosity:
   Holy Spirit increase our tenderness and kindness.
Let us pray in gratitude for the gift of sexual union:
   Holy Spirit enflame the fire of our passion.
Let us pray for sexual sensitivity and courtesy:
   Holy Spirit warm us with sexual joy and happiness.

Prayer:
God who created us in your image and then becomes incarnate to join humankind, help us to affirm the goodness of our embodied selves. Make us grateful and joyful in our sexual powers and pleasures. Let our sexual desires and loving always give you glory. Thank you for the sexual gifts and fruits that bring joy, comfort, healing, union and increase love in our marriage. Amen.

CHAPTER FIVE

• MOTHERING •

Becoming a mother
Only an event like the Big Bang equals the exciting and exhausting drama of giving birth to a new human being. Becoming a mother creates a relationship with a new life that can never be undone. The world is forever changed. At this awe-inspiring event, a mother can be overwhelmed by the flood of emotions. Joy and intense happiness make the heart soar, but anxiety also appears. Fear of the unknown may bring disturbing questions. Will I be able to give my child a good life? Can I protect my baby in the face of the larger world's unpredictable forces?

The crucial importance of mothering for a child's life is no longer in doubt. New knowledge of infancy and child development reveals how high the maternal stakes are. Lifelong consequences of every kind depend upon the nurturing provided by a mother from conception on throughout childhood. Adult health consequences, for instance, are now being attributed to fetal and infant nutrition and care. Physical survival and the healthy development of body, brain and intelligence depend on adequate feeding, vigilant protection and appropriate stimulation. A child's personal and social development may be even more powerfully affected by early experiences of caretaking.

As mothers attentively respond to their children they are shaping their personalities and emotional responsiveness to other human beings. Tender and prompt responses to the baby's needs demonstrate to an infant that the world is a good and safe place where you always get what is necessary and where others respond to you and your signals. Soothing verbal responses, eye-to-eye gaze, tender touch and embracing, supportive arms give babies a sense of security.

Evolutionary Preparation for Mothering

Mothers and babies are innately prepared by millions of years of evolutionary selection to play their roles. Women and babies come into the world with innate developmental programs that are ready to be triggered and activated. Mothers have built in responses while giving birth and are able to nurse, comfort and playfully interact with their infants. Babies possess remarkable intuitive capacities to become attached to their mothers, acquire language rules, number concepts and logical reasoning. But perhaps the most valuable innate capacity that human infants develop is the powerful ability to love and emotionally relate to others appropriately and skillfully.

The discovery of attachment and innately developing social intelligence in children has been an exciting research project. Chimpanzees may be pretty intelligent but humans excel in developing the social skills of reading other humans' minds and emotions, even before their unique gifts of language blossom. Humans develop a theory of mind that operates in understanding others. Persons' intentions and emotions are recognized by their facial gestures, postures, vocalizations and other signals. And all of this preverbal behavior begins in infancy.

Naturally, it is a great advantage for both defensive survival and altruistic cooperation when individuals can understand and predict other people's intentions and responses. And, as the theory holds, in developing this social intelligence you discover and develop your own self awareness. Each personal self appears to come into full consciousness through interpersonal relationships with others. Social communication, beginning with mother and child, produces individuality.

In the last decades, infant studies and neuroscientists have made remarkable discoveries of the way human communication operates. It is not only the case that all of the different senses bring information in and send signals out. More remarkably, mirror neuron systems in the brain have been found by which humans mirror in their own brains the actions and reactions they observe in others. As discussed in previous chapters here, mirror responses mean that human beings can directly feel what another is feeling. Empathy, or feeling with another, is a crucial human capacity.

This direct experiential sharing of empathy and mirroring of others' responses is the basis of imitation and learning, but also of emotional communication. Emotions have always been known to be contagious; you cry and tears come to my eyes, you laugh and I laugh, you panic and I am afraid as well. The power of empathy also makes moral responses to another possible because I feel as you feel and can treat you as I would be treated.

Infants cry when other babies cry and toddlers try to comfort others in distress. Normal human beings come with the neurological equipment to innately participate in others' emotions and responses. The mysterious sense of loving intersubjective communion and shared interpersonal space with others, now is known to have a neurological base in human brains.

These innate abilities enable humans to decode the subtle nonverbal cues from other faces, postures, gestures, touch, vocalizations and tones of voice. Attentive mothers sense what their babies and children are feeling and vice versa. Human communication consists of far more channels than words and speech. Mothers and babies commune from the beginning through empathy, emotional understanding, shared attention to objects and shared activities. Mutual eye-gazing, for instance, conveys mother-infant love, and shifting gaze regulates interactions in subtle ways.

A loving dialogue or dance of adjustment takes place between mothers and babies, indeed within all person-to-person encounters. Smooth interactions and appropriately tuned responses give each party the feeling of a harmonious and satisfactory interchange.

With babies and children the process of giving and receiving loving attention builds up the bonds of love. These bonds establish the secure identity of a self. When no one responds to your overture there is always a sense of discord and dissonance.

Affectionate playing with babies is also important, not only for the stimulation and practice in human interaction, but because it releases the innate joy that humans take in mutual intimacy and interaction. To know and be known, to love and be loved—these are the goods human seek from the beginning to the end of life.

Human social groups make babies a focus of interest and attention. The protective instinct is strong and an infant's cry motivates a rescue response. Members of a group, including older children, innately know how to play with babies and take joy in the play. With babies a special voice and tone is used to communicate effectively, with special exaggerated human facial expressions. Baby talk exists in every language.

Others have thought that the way a baby looks, with big eyes, round cheeks and forehead, is a "baby schema" or pattern that innately releases positive and protective human responses. Dolls, dogs and cartoon figures are more attractive when babylike. Mickey Mouse's face became more infantile over successive generations, more like a baby and less like a rat.

Each infant and child's existence will be embedded in an extended social network of kin and neighbors that can further its survival. A child is a link to its parents' families and kinship groups; human groups are enlivened and blessed by their new infants and children. As the old saying goes, it takes a village to rear a child—and truly appreciate and delight in a child. Unfortunately, it is also possible for the complex processes of childbirth and rearing to go wrong for many reasons which we will discuss below. But more generally, evolutionary selection processes support the great developmental project that produces human beings.

A mother may love her baby for itself, as a fruit of her body, as a gift of love from her husband and as a link to her own family and clan. These emotional investments of love and interest invoke the capacity for human growth and flourishing. Mothers are privileged to be the central figure in each human drama. "All generations shall call me blessed," sings Mary in her great hymn of praise, the Magnificat. Mary in her part in the Incarnation has been given a unique role, but other mothers can echo her song of joyful purpose.

Maternal Love

Love is the basic human emotion that emerges early in infancy as the fusion of joy and interest; it can then be richly developed and last for all of life. As discussed in earlier chapters, love affirms, celebrates and says yes to what is loved. Lovers unite with the valued loved ones and desire to serve their good. Maternal love shares in the essential character of all love and is a particularly privileged and powerful way of loving. It may also be the fiercest of all loving, as evidence from the animal kingdom attests.

Human love is considered an innate basic emotion that is a fusion of joy and interest. It emerges early in infancy and grows in response to a mother's love. Maternal altruism and self-giving are called forth in the loving of her infant. There is an intense motivation to protect, care for and rejoice in her baby. A mother's love is emotionally intense, tender, joyful and unconditionally committed to the child's well being.

When all goes well, the infant responds with love and becomes attached to its mother. The bonds of love between mother and child can become deeper and stronger as an escalating dialogue of empathy and appropriate response take place. One joy of maternal love is being able to meet a child's needs and desires. So too, a child's woe and pain will be felt deeply by the empathetic mother, but often a mother can alleviate her child's distress.

Love for children can be wonderfully concrete, embodied, necessary and effective. Love is demonstrated by acts of caretaking that are necessary and obvious. The baby is hungry and must be fed, she is dirty and must be bathed, diapered, dressed, played with, soothed and put to sleep—over and over again. In affluent countries, babies are taken to doctor appointments and on outings that require being put in and out of high-tech equipment. Each activity of caretaking can be done in a tender, gentle, playful manner that expresses maternal affection and affirmation.

Maternal love is privileged in being so basic and concrete. Christians can rejoice in imitating Christ humbly washing the feet of his disciples. All of the works of mercy held up in the gospels such as feeding the hungry or clothing the naked can be performed in caring for children. All of the great Christian saints have found concrete ways to love their neighbor in their loving of God. Saint Thérèse of Lisieux described her "little way" of doing the smallest daily acts in her convent with the greatest of love. She would pick up a pin or smile at a crosspatch nun with intense loving kindness. She has always inspired me as a model for the mothering way of love. Little bits of behavior, or micro acts of love, can be done with large-hearted intentions.

Other spiritual masters speak of living and loving through "the sacrament of the present moment." Whatever is happening this minute can be met with God's loving response. Nothing is too small or too concrete to be done with love. Now is the only time we actually have to love and serve. "Do what you are doing," is another spiritual counsel drawing on the same wisdom. Mothers caring for children and doing the same repetitive chores of maintaining house and home can raise their hearts in practicing the little way in the present moment.

Family life has been called the school of Christian love for a reason. Moment by moment another's need or a pressing task is encountered in maternal life. An opportunity is presented to give and respond with love: Yes, let me do thy will, and with glad generosity. All of the fruits of the Spirit can be invoked: let me be full of joy, love, humility, kindness, gentleness, patience, self-control and generosity. Patience, peacefulness and perseverance may be the hardest responses for mothers to acquire in frantic, ever-rushing stress-filled societies.

While true maternal love is given and enjoyed as its own reward, a beloved child is blessed, secure and blossoms in the light and warmth of her mother's love. Body, mind and spirit are so intertwined that maternal love benefits a child's physical health as well as her intellectual, emotional and social intelligence. A beloved child who is securely attached to her mother is free to respond with playful delight and interest to the environment. She trusts that all will be well and so can invest in what has been called "the child's love affair with the world."

As children pursue lively playful discoveries of the world, adults can relive their own early experiences. To vicariously see the world afresh gives new energy to distracted and busy adults. The great gift of loving babies and children is sharing in their wonder and joy; it renews an adult's own childlike delight in the good and the beautiful. Psychological observers have noted that the process of birthing and rearing a child gives a mother an impetus to grow, enrich and open up her own personality to the new.

Most appropriately, the image of a new baby symbolizes hope and the advent of renewal. Mother and child give promise of love and the joyful coming of the new. Moreover, a little child has been held up as a spiritual mentor in the kingdom. Children live in the present, give their love and trust, play and rejoice in the world. Christians understand why Jesus wanted the children to come to him—accompanied by their mothers of course.

Those who love and care for children can have their hearts enlarged, refreshed and gladdened. If women on the whole seem more benevolent than men, it can be because they give birth and spend so much time intimately caring for children. At least women in western societies seem to become freer to spontaneously express joy and playfulness. Or perhaps it is a function of the way power and humility are most often distributed between men and women. Power invites efforts to control and dominate while maternal love inspires humility and generosity. Moreover, the merry comic element of life is more in evidence in the kitchen and nursery than in the executive suite.

Mothers get used to keeping a loving eye out for the needs of everyone else in the environment; it is almost a sixth sense which can't be turned off. Surely it is easier to grow in self-giving sensitive love in a life with children. A childless young professional, sometimes even a cleric, may seem somewhat tone deaf to others or rather seriously self-focused. Great celibate saints seemed to have solved the problem by reproducing the demands of maternal love and family needs in their lives. They end up giving the same kind of day and night commitment and unconditional love that children receive. Their titles of "Mother" or "Father" are well earned.

While the unconditional maternal love given a child values the child just as they are, mothers and fathers are also charged in love to help their children grow up. Parents have to prepare their children to become mature enough to become adults who can themselves love and be good parents. The love given to a child must aim to be transforming love that gently tutors, encourages or nudges children to increase in grace and wisdom.

Some correction of a child will be necessary. Some friction is usually part of the socializing process parents must undertake. A child or adolescent will resist and a necessary separation and distancing must begin in order for a child to become independent. In these difficult encounters, antagonism and some aggression can be vented upon mothers. These hard times test the unconditional commitment of parental love. To love when being rejected means that you must remain steadfast and benevolent in the face of hostile attack. It is the supreme test for mothering, one in which Christ's command to return love is required—even when you are rejected and hated. One's offspring may be only an intimate enemy for a temporary period, but the challenge of loving wisely and truly remains.

Morally, all mothers are obliged to fulfill their vocation to love in their roles as stewards, guides, guardians, coaches and teachers. They must be models and exemplars in order to demonstrate and give the kind of love that is required. You can't give what you don't have so mothers have to grow in love. You can only teach what you know; so mothers seek wisdom so that they can pass on their legacy of Christian culture and civilization.

Maternal Thinking

Mothers who love their children need to think well and make good decisions about their welfare. This kind of strategic forethought has been called "maternal thinking." Traditionally it could be seen as an exercise of practical wisdom or prudence, that is, doing the best thing in a particular set of circumstances in the best possible way. Such thinking is not necessarily gender specific, but mothers usually take on this responsibility since they spend more time and pay more attention to a child than anyone else.

Good maternal thinking has been analyzed as having three main functions: first, to protect a child from harm; second, to have the child flourish as an individual; and third, to raise a child that is acceptable to society and able to function in it as an adult. Protecting is a large order in a complex society with various tasks ranging from babyproofing houses full of electrical outlets and poisons to procuring inoculations and ensuring outdoor safety in and from cars. Wild animals are usually no longer a problem in modern neighborhoods but other human predators can be on the scene.

To help a child flourish as an individual, the freedom to fulfill personal desires and talents has to be encouraged. But children at the same time have to learn to behave, to be educated and generally follow the society's rules if they are to become acceptable members of their society. Otherwise they will be ostracized and grow up not being able to find work, support themselves, marry or begin families of their own.

Unfortunately, in an imperfect world the different maternal goals will be in conflict with one another. Expressing and fulfilling a child's personal desires and talents may endanger their safety and threaten their social acceptability. Enforcing social conformity in a child may suppress individual creative fulfillment. Conflicting alternatives have to be weighed in order to make good decisions.

Mothers have to *think* through their larger long-term goals and in conditions of uncertainty choose a course of action to the best of their ability. This is why high intelligence in a loving mature mother is such an advantage for a child. Balancing the benefits and costs of different goals and the effectiveness of the means to get there is a perennial challenge. Flexibility and responding to change is important; there are few blueprints or all-purpose handbooks.

Each child and family and set of circumstances is different so no automatic rule will apply. Women with logical, emotional and social intelligence will think long and hard but also seek the good counsel of others. Good advice can come from every source and different kinds of expertise called upon that can help a child. Prejudice against psychological help is as misguided as discounting medical advice. All resources are helpful and need to be weighed and synthesized.

In the overall struggle to weigh all factors and make good decisions, mothers will do well as always to look to the wise and good and seek the counsel of the Holy Spirit. The Spirit of God gives wisdom and knowledge. Christians can test every spirit by looking to the traditions of the church, to the Scriptures and to God's gifts of reason and experience.

Mothers also turn to their own mothers and their supportive female kin and friends. Networks of women have helped mothers of every age and stage. Grandmothers who love their grandchildren, as the children of their children, can also be wellsprings of wisdom and maternal thinking. Older women who have seen cycles of medical and maternal advice come and go, can achieve a more balanced view of what is really important and essential and what is less so.

For Christians, moral and religious formation and education is always essential. Much maternal wisdom is called for in guiding a child's moral and religious development. Yes, Christian parents want to raise children who are acceptable to their peers and their society, but even more they want their children to be devoted to God's kingdom and the church.

Here there can be a perennial conflict faced by mothers in the struggle against a materialistic, aggressive society on behalf of Christian justice and love of neighbor. Mothers who work for peace and the welfare of the poor will not be satisfied with a child's worldly materialistic success. A child has to be given the strength to judge the world by higher Christian standards.

Mothers want to have children who are not only functioning members of society but who are also virtuous and do good. Few greater moments of pride and joy arrive in life than sharing in an upstanding child's success in doing good work for others. They do not have to be heroic martyrs but must be morally good men and women.

By contrast, nothing hurts quite so much as being disappointed in a child's moral failure. In the Bible, King David is poignantly described as weeping and mourning over the betrayal of his son, Absalom. "Oh Absalom, Absalom, my son Absalom."

Christian parents will continue to love an erring child but the pain can be great. The greater the gifts of a child, the more sorrow experienced when they are not fulfilled.

Admittedly, parents want to have morally good children partially for self-interested reasons. Avoiding parental shame, disappointment and sense of failure is an understandable motivation. Another reason is the half-unconscious desire of raising a conscientious child who will honor and care for his parents, when they are old and in need of help. Inevitably, adult children will eventually have to assume obligations for long lived fragile parents.

A good-hearted moral child will be responsible and give nurturing care. In an earlier day the elderly had to rely upon their adult children for food and shelter, but in an affluent society it is more a matter of giving time and attentive love. Adult children "honor their father and mother" by visiting, running errands and dealing with health care providers.

Americans live so long that years of reverse parenting can be called for. The tenfold increase of Alzheimer's disease is imposing a further need for caretaking on families. Nurturing older parents replays the loving care given to the young at the beginning of life. Middle-aged mothers in our society are also daughters. They can be seen on any given day ministering to their parents in the nation's nursing homes and dementia wards. They have not abandoned the old or let them go.

A paradoxical challenge of maternal love and thinking in regard to one's growing children is to be able to give children their freedom and independence to go forth, but also to become the kind of persons that will care for their parents when the need arises. Letting children go is imperative in order for them to flourish as adults and find their own way to serve the world. But then, while the goal is to raise a good, independent, equal adult person, one desires to have a child who affirms the words of the old Baptist hymn: "Blessed be the tie that binds."

Jesus himself castigated those hypocritical religious adults who did not support their aging parents. And in the midst of his tortured death Christ commends Mary to the care of his disciple John. Jesus knew that his universal mission to the world had to take him away from home and the family, but he continues to love and care for his mother. Christ applies to himself the image of a mother hen longing to protect her chicks under her wing, so he understands what mothering love and thinking is all about. He is rightly known to mystics as Christ Our Mother.

Maternal Dangers and Obstacles

Mothers currently face many kinds of danger which cause concern. Media alerts have sounded over the problem of women's depression and in particular post-partum depression. The worldwide scourge of depression afflicts more women than men, but no one is spared—the affluent, the poor, the old and the young suffer.

It is a double tragedy however, when a new mother becomes depressed and withdraws into sadness and numbed apathy; her baby loses its responsive nurturing partner in a critical period. Mother's attentive care is needed to give babies and children a sense of security as well as ensuring the development of emotional, cognitive and social intelligence.

It is one thing to experience a brief bout of the "Baby Blues" arising from emotional overload, but a seriously depressed new mother needs to be helped as soon as possible. Children are resilient, but a good beginning is crucial to later well being.

Other maternal dangers for both mother and child arise from physical illness, accidents and other misfortunes. The entangled condition of mother and child welfare begins in fetal life and lasts throughout childhood and adolescence. A mother's alcohol or drug addiction, for instance, can impair her fetal child's chances for normalcy. Addiction or mental illness during a child's early and later years will be destructive to the family.

Family well being depends upon a mother's physical and emotional health, upon her intelligence and moral maturity. Self-giving altruism may be the norm, but a woman's selfishness or weakness of character do not automatically disappear when she has a child.

The demands for maternal altruism that babies bring can deplete or overwhelm a fragile mother's personal and moral resources. Colicky babies, impaired or sick children can increase the pressure on a mother's stable functioning. Empathy fatigue can set in with its corresponding temptation to neglect the needs of a child.

Impaired maternal functioning arises from many sources. An immature or frustrated mother may succumb to weakness of will and the desire to escape. Existing character flaws may be exacerbated and result in neglectful mothering. The more external pressure and internal weakness present, the more likelihood of maternal failure. There is a dark shadowed side to the story of children's fate. Their complete vulnerability and helplessness, along with their need for constant care, has made maltreatment possible and frequent.

While the evolutionary story is generally positive, there is also the fact that infanticide, child abandonment and exploitative child abuse is part of the evil human heritage. Children can be maltreated and abused by mothers as well as by aggressive males. Personal inadequacies interact with ignorance, low intelligence and stressful negative circumstances can activate cruelty.

Impairments from drug or alcohol addictions affect children's fate in the family. When maternal protection breaks down children are at risk. Maternal mistreatment and abuse of children is a dreadful reality. "Mommy dearests" and other monstrous mothers do exist and inflict lasting psychological and physical harm upon children. Jesus said that it would be better to have a millstone around your neck than to suffer the fate of those who abuse children (see Matthew 18:6). Unfortunately, mothers can be among these sinners.

However one does not have to consider only extreme negative cases to see other dangers and obstacles for mothers. Basically good mothers can also fail their children in times of stress. An exhausted, hard-pressed mother may give in to a selfish desire for relief, or flare up aggressively in reaction to frustration. The relentless demand to put another's needs before your own can provoke occasional rebellion. The greedy infantile ego surges forth in imperfect personalities.

The most loving of mothers can have moments when they rebel or break down. Isolation and lack of support can be oppressive. The struggle to sustain love's self-control and patience has its momentary defeats. Mothers of impaired, mentally disturbed or chronically ill children face heroic demands—and even more so if they live in poverty or are single.

On the other hand, well-favored and fortunate parents can face other more subtle dangers. Mothers who have energy, intelligence, material resources and strong wills can give way to obsessive drives to produce the perfect child. Today affluent parents can be guilty of "hyper-parenting" as they pursue what has been called "the mission." The mission is an all-out effort to push children to succeed in competitive academic and athletic activities.

I know of a highly educated immigrant family who are actually having their delightful fourth-grade daughter tutored for the SATs, so that she can get into Yale and then go to Harvard Medical School. Every weekday this child is chauffeured to a musical, athletic or intellectual enrichment program. Her success will be defined by high achievement that is financially rewarded.

This parental mission aimed at worldly success more or less ignores the civic sphere of achieving the common good or meeting the needs of the poor for health care and social justice. Larger ideals and altruistic concerns become subordinated to the private good of the individual and the family. Money will buy pleasures, goods and security. In the super-competitive American race for success, pressures and stress mount for harried mothers and hurried children.

The danger is that the goal becomes centered more on parental success at competitive childrearing than on the moral well being and flourishing of the children and a good society. The Promethean drive for mastery and perfection is privatized and spiritually harmful. Christian mothers must struggle against these subtle forms of selfishness. And how? By example and the creative affirmation of serving one's neighbor.

All of those good things in our society that engender altruism among the young must be experienced by children. Soup kitchens and peace demonstrations, visits to nursing homes and cleaning up the environment—all of these activities must be encouraged. Mothers who are on God's mission must open their children's eyes and let empathy have its own potent effect.

Christian Affirmations of Mothering

Christian mothers can be guarded from many ills by their beliefs about the larger purpose of having children. All life and everything we do is co-creating the new earth and new heaven. Children are not meant to be our possessions but are gifts, here to be loved and lived with on a shared journey to God. Our children should be accepted in hospitable love as fellow pilgrims on the way. They deserve from us all the best resources we can muster to help them grow and mature. Christian love for children, like all love, treats the other with empathy, intimate interest and commitment to just treatment.

Our investment in children is not made in a utilitarian calculus to reap benefits, such as paybacks in old age, or to get grandchildren or receive worldly praise. Rather, to have and rear a child is a privilege because it gives a concrete opportunity for an intense enduring human bond of kinship and love. Certainly, it is not even about having the uplifting experience of childbirth and childrearing as the ultimate consumer good. Mothers and fathers also are not engaged in the ultimate achievement project to obtain perfection and control of lives—theirs, mine and ours together.

The Christian brief against perfection argues that a drive for mastery and control escalates and will end in destructive consequences for those being controlled, as well as for the controllers. To love means living serenely and happily, remaining open to the unbidden in life's journey. The acceptance of mutual imperfection in family life is a mark of true love's humility. Humility accepts limits in self and others. The great child psychologist Donald Woods Winnicott spoke of the "good enough mother," and thereby freed many modern women from self-flagellation and guilt over their imperfections.

Those filled with proud and competitive drives for perfection should not be working them out on their children. As already mentioned, the dynamic American can-do culture of competition, mastery, consumption and control is exerting escalating pressures on parents, children and the schools. It is a sign of the times that high schools in ambitious achieving suburbs should be instituting stress reduction campaigns to relieve the anxiety of students. These programs are often adopted after adolescent suicides occur.

How much more beneficial it would be for Christians to be teaching their children the art of meditation and contemplative prayer! There is much need for young people to be inducted into their own western spiritual traditions of prayer. To learn to be receptive to God's love and presence will be important for everything encountered in the future.

Christians affirm that each life is a gift which cannot be morally manipulated to another's specific standards at any stage. Parents who have determined to be perfect parents and raise the perfect child are not listening to the lessons of history, religion or human experience. When you read Scripture, literature, biography, psychology and look around at the families that you know, it becomes evident that there are no guarantees in childbearing or childrearing.

Environmental and chance social forces combine with intentional individual decisions to shape lives in unpredictable ways. With their understanding of the primacy of altruistic self-giving love, Christians can accept and bear patiently the extra burdens of disabled children. Impairments or mental and moral failures in their children do not extinguish altruistic love. A mother who loves is doing God's own work of loving nurture and co-creating.

Christians call God Our Mother because God, like a mother, gives us life and love—and also leaves us free to grow into our own strength. No coercion or control can bring forth a freely chosen maturity. No mother wants to have a puppet like Pinocchio for a child. A living child must be nurtured and given freedom. Mothers want adult children to be equal friends and maturely competent. God calls disciples to grow up into Christ and be transformed.

When children do succeed and grow up into loving adults, Christian parents know that it is not their doing alone. The wonderful God-given potentialities for development of the human being have been elicited and released by love's labor won. To have wonderful good children is the greatest of all joys, but it is not really so much an achievement as a blessing bestowed. To watch one's children become good and loving parents to their own children is an ultimate delight.

Christians who have known the good news of Christ's resurrection know that a new heaven and new earth is being created here and now. Whatever one does in the most ordinary way in family life is contributing to the larger divine drama of transforming this world into the kingdom. No act is too small or trivial. Every diaper changed, dish washed, every smiling caress, every word or act, along with every irritable response that is restrained will serve God's loving purpose. Does this understanding increase the responsibility of being a mother?

Yes, but there is a comforting side to the understanding of the drama. I am not alone in my efforts. I too am a child of God and beloved by Christ and the cloud of witnesses that surround us. Every support of the Holy Spirit and the church is available for me and mine. Mary, the Mother of God, prays for mothers and their children. I am not the sole possessor of my child, because I receive this child as a gift to be held in trust.

The whole creation from its beginning has been evolving in order to enable this new member of the human family to be and to become. God loves by Self-spending, by giving life to others and by letting others be uniquely themselves. In the end mothers do the same. A mother is a created "cocreator." There is no self-made person and there is no self-sufficient individual who can flourish alone. Happiness must always consist of relations with others, for it is what has been called a "together good." Only being with the other can give the surprise and unexpected response that delights. And all of this human happiness, joy and playfulness begins at birth. Mothers cocreate and help bring joy to the world.

FOOD FOR THOUGHT

1. If you are a mother in either a literal or figurative sense, have you been conscious of the wonderful ways that love between mother and child helps create a new person? How do you experience nonverbal empathy and communion with children?

2. What gifts and fruits of the Holy Spirit have helped you in mothering? What are some instances of maternal thinking that you have employed in raising children at different stages of family life?
3. What dangers have you encountered in your experiences as a mother? What temptations have been most difficult to withstand?
4. The word *mother* refers to more than persons who physically bear a child. How does the word *mother* as a metaphor point to the call of everyone to be a mothering one?

Prayer

Invocation:
God Our Mother,
   Give birth to us anew.
God Our Mother,
   Deepen our loving.
God Our Mother,
   Transform us.

Scripture: Isaiah 66:10–14; Luke 13:34

Response:
Let us be grateful for our long journey of evolution that prepares us to give birth and nurture new lives:
   Christ Our Mother feed us.
Let us pray for prudence and wisdom to make good decisions in our mothering:
   Christ Our Mother let us grow up in you.
Let us pray for strength to be humble and accept imperfections in ourselves as we do in our children:
   Christ Our Mother forgive us as we forgive others.

Prayer:

Holy Spirit who begets us and nurtures our growth, help us to value each child of God as God does. Give us courage and strength to overcome every obstacle and temptation through love. We seek courage and perseverance in order to hope in you. Amen.

CHAPTER SIX

• WOMEN AND WORK •

American women in this fast-paced and high-pressure society must make decisions about work under new circumstances. More married women with children are educated and have access to work and careers outside of the home. At the same time childrearing grows more demanding—and more expensive. Should mothers work, or continue to work?

Many women who are caught in poverty or hard pressed financially have little choice; they must have paid employment in order to provide food and shelter for their families. If there is an economic slump and families are threatened with losing their homes, more women will feel pressure to bring in income. As times worsen, women have difficulties getting or keeping their jobs.

Yet at the other end of the spectrum, highly affluent and educated women are voluntarily dropping out of the workforce to stay home and rear their children. Other women in the middle ranges of family earning power also make voluntary decisions to forgo working for pay. They manage by adopting lifestyles that sacrifice many of the usual consumer goods and luxuries. Families committed to home-centered lives of frugal self-reliance may move to less expensive locales or join likeminded communities. Many women acting upon their ideological and religious commitments may not only stay home, but home school their children.

The range and variety of women's options concerning work occasions a multitude of voices offering advice and admonitions. Since the beginning of the women's movement in the '60s the topic of combining women's work and family life has been central. Magazine articles, books, columns, media programs and learned research studies are constantly coming out putting forth different messages which often conflict. The arguments in these offerings are implicitly shaped by underlying assumptions and value judgments about what is most important in life. These values need to be discerned and addressed. Christian women will want to have clarity and understand the contexts of the issues that reflect different spiritual perspectives on work.

Psychosocial insights and findings can also be helpful when considering these contested issues of work. Since individuals and social circumstances differ radically, and families are always changing, no rule can ever apply rigidly to all women at every stage of their working lives. In the brief exploration below, I begin with some reflections on Christian attitudes toward work and then go on to pertinent psychological and experiential considerations that can be helpful in making decisions.

In my own married life the question of combining work with family has always presented acute moral, religious and practical dilemmas. Early in my writing career I wrote a book called *The Working Mother* (1968) laying out different theories and the existing research on the subject, followed by interviews with women who had worked while rearing their children. I wrote one of the chapters under a pseudonym in order to express my own conflicts. On the whole I was trying to give voice to my resistance to the then-reigning "feminine mystique" and cult of "the eternal feminine" which disapproved of women's careers outside the home. But I also had doubts and anxieties about leaving the house even for part-time study.

As a young bride in the late '50s I had encountered a priest who had castigated my plan to gradually procure a graduate education in order to teach when my children were older. "Well," said my clerical critic, "Be sure and lay aside money from your salary to pay for the psychiatrist your children will need." What an assault on a newly married wife without any babies yet, or for that matter any funds for tuition until my husband finished *his* GI Bill studies, that, as it turned out, would take nine years of living below the poverty line. Remembering this conversation helps recall the strength of the 1950s consensus that mothers should never work, if they could possibly avoid it. For that matter married women were not allowed into graduate programs and might be dismissed from teaching in a Catholic college on marriage. Those of us who were trying to develop a Christian feminist approach to women's equality of opportunity faced an uphill road.

Naturally, after living through those earlier struggles, I have been fascinated to see the resurgence of the arguments between two fiercely opposing positions on women's employment. On the one hand there is a resurgence of a feisty feminist pro-career message to women, and on the other, a vigorous pro-homemaking position that is gaining adherents among young women. The media dubs this fracas, "the mommy wars." Obviously, arguments over combining family and work have not gone away. Taking account of the differing arguments and arriving at a workable Christian synthesis is still a challenge. Weighing the issues and struggling to arrive at good decisions may be so difficult because competing goods are involved. How should Christians view their priorities on work and on what grounds?

A Christian Perspective on Women's Work

The Scriptures convey Jesus' challenging words, "From everyone to whom much has been given, much will be required; and from the one to whom much has been entrusted, even more will be demanded" (Luke 12:48). This clearly implies that women who have personal talents, capacities and cultural resources have a moral obligation to use them well. In acts of good stewardship, resources and talents are not to be buried away but to be used, developed and increased. Not surprisingly, the responsibility to use personal gifts worthily is recognized as a moral obligation in every moral and ethical system. Does a Christian theological perspective on work, virtue and the use of gifts go further? I think so.

Christians affirm that all honest work is valuable because it imitates and participates in God's creative work. God as Creator makes heaven and earth and all things visible and invisible; God sees that the work is good. Indeed, God is continually creating and sustaining the world. The whole creation is dynamically moving toward God's future fulfillment of a new heaven and a new earth. Christians as God's good stewards and coworkers are called to take care and to develop the new creation that God is bringing to fruition.

Christ's disciples will participate in his work of saving and healing the wounds of the disordered and incomplete evolving world. The future goal is a kingdom of justice, truth and joy where God is all in all. When Jesus defends his healing of the paralytic on the Sabbath, he proclaims "My Father is still working, and I also am working" (John 5:17). God in Christ works and desires God's children to be fellow workers in setting right what is wrong, developing what is potential and helping God's kingdom come on earth, as it is in heaven.

Whatever Christians do in word and deed can be offered for God's glory (Colossians 3:17). The harvest awaits and no effort by faithful workers, no matter how small, will be wasted or lost. The cup of water given, the widow's mite offered at the temple, the anointing of the prophet's head and washing his feet— every loving work of feeding and clothing, sowing and harvesting, will bear fruit. This privileged role of co-creating with, in and through Christ gives meaning to every human act, whether small or large, joyful or painful.

In this disordered world painful human drudgery is often necessary for survival. Punitive work beats people down and wears them out. But even coerced work, even the suffering work of slaves and prisoners can be offered to build the kingdom. Nothing is futile. Christ's victory over death in the Resurrection produces the first fruits of the new world in which heaven and earth are joined to ensure that every tear will be wiped away. The victory which is "already," is slowly moving toward the "not yet," the yeast is active and the bread is rising.

Christians work out their salvation in a world that is being transformed, as Christ's risen body is already transformed. This is good news not only about the usefulness of all work, but also because it confers value and worth on every worker, no matter how humble. Women can be particularly assured that their labor to meet the needs of their children or neighbors is a form of love in action that bears much fruit. Theirs can be the hidden and "little way" of doing every task and service inspired by love. Saint Thérèse of Lisieux in her convent aspiring to the little way, would patiently work in the splashing laundry line and graciously help old cranky nuns to their dinner. Young mothers in their hidden work may have things much easier because feeding, bathing and comforting children can be pleasurable.

Christians also are enjoined to work to achieve self-sufficiency. Paul proudly boasts that he has provided for his needs by the work of his hands and not been a burden upon his followers. An aristocratic disdain for physical work has no place for those who follow a God who becomes flesh and humbly lives to serve others. Paul's praise of a hardy work ethic is true to Christ's teaching. Long ago when our house was filled with lazy teenagers, we posted Paul's dictum on the refrigerator door: "Anyone unwilling to work should not eat" (2 Thessalonians 3:10). Christians expect that every able-bodied member of the community should be willing to perform wholehearted, steadfast and careful work for themselves and the common good.

The valorization of good work in Christianity appeared from the first disciples and continued on into the medieval Benedictine motto "to work is to pray," and on to modern French worker priests and members of Dorothy Day's Catholic worker houses. In recent papal encyclicals and Catholic social teaching, human work is esteemed as morally good—because of the intention of the worker, because of work's capacity to provide for the needs of self and others, and because it is building the renewed kingdom to come.

Disciples can know that work of every kind is the way to effectively show love and mercy to others. The faithful will follow Christ's example of washing his follower's feet and his call to serve rather than be served. All of the traditional works of mercy are aimed at actively meeting the needs of those in distress, or in want of physical or psychological help. From feeding the hungry to comforting the sorrowful to instructing the ignorant and admonishing the sinful, the goal of work is to help your neighbor. How closely the works of mercy fit the daily efforts of every mother in her household.

Out of the home, Christian women working for justice engage in public and community efforts for the "civilization of love," held up as the goal in Catholic social doctrine. In service of the common good, physical, social and intellectual labor is needed: to set the unjust world to rights and allow humans to flourish. An impartial God of justice and truth commands worshipers to work toward righteousness, honesty and equality in all things. But it should not be forgotten that the God of justice is also the God of beauty, music, joy and truth.

God is glorified by creative, artistic, intellectual and scientific work. Human gifts of reason employed in science, medicine and invention can produce great accomplishments and works of mercy in the world. Women as disciples are called to dream dreams and take part in every creative work.

But if work of every kind is affirmed—whether chosen or coerced, fulfilling or punitive, great or small, physical or intellectual—then how does a disciple decide which work to pursue? Women can know that their unique capacity for creating life through childbearing and traditional family caretaking gives glory to God, but so do women's labors for others, for self-sufficiency, for justice, for truth and for beauty. While every good work can build up the kingdom on earth and in the world to come, every good work cannot be pursued in one embodied and limited lifetime. Which work should a woman undertake?

Here the scriptural teaching on the variation of talents and gifts can be helpful. The unique talents, capacities and resources that disciples possess as their genetic and social heritage can be a guide to the work that they can pursue well. According to Paul, there are many different parts of the body that are equally valuable, and in the same way there are many different talents and capacities for work that are equally valuable and acceptable to God. In one charming medieval fable, a simple juggler spends the night in church offering his juggling skills as a gift to God and Our Lady. Mary rewards his night's work by appearing and wiping the sweat from his brow.

The lesson of the story is the same message as that of the gorgeously crafted medieval cathedral. God wills that human talents should be used creatively for beauty and joy. It should always be remembered that Jesus was full of joyful eagerness to do his Father's work, which he described as his meat and drink. Jesus promises also that his disciples with the aid of his spirit will do greater work than he (John 14:12). Learning from Christ's example, his followers are to go and do likewise. The word, likewise, is important because it does not narrow a disciple's work to an exactly detailed imitation. Disciples need not choose to be a carpenter, or a teaching rabbi or an unjustly crucified victim of an imperial regime; but disciples are meant to work in the spirit of Jesus, whatever they do.

Another helpful way of choosing work is to read the signs of the times, that is to assess the unique circumstances prevailing in the present. For instance, what is happening around you and what state of life have you already embraced through a previous commitment? The traditional concept of being guided by your state of life refers to those obligations and commitments a person may already have undertaken, such as marriage or parenthood or religious vows. Once obligations to others exist they cannot simply be dismissed or disregarded. Once one has children, for example, they possess claims to having their needs met.

At this point an all-time worst example of a misguided motherhood irresistibly comes to mind, Charles Dickens's notorious Mrs. Jellyby from *Bleak House*. This energetic lady continually and completely ignores her brood of ill-fed, ill-clothed, unwashed and wailing children in order to work day and night on committees to save the orphans of Africa. This tragicomic figure has entertained generations of readers of fiction, but who has not encountered similar cases in real life? In earlier decades when married lay activity in the church was first being promoted, certain caustic remarks could be bandied about referring to "Catholic action orphans."

Jesus himself rebuked the religious hypocrites of his day who neglected to support their older parents while ostentatiously giving money to the temple. As the first letter of John reiterates, anyone who claims to love God whom you cannot see, while refusing to love those you *can* see, is a liar (1 John 4:20). Obviously, a woman's moral obligation to care for her dependent children must remain primary in career decisions. But just as obviously, this obligation can be well-fulfilled in different ways. It is possible to meet several sets of compatible obligations in a day. (More on this below.)

In addition to being guided by states of life and individual talents, persons also are led to vocations by external chance contingencies. Caught in a civil war, or a famine, or a plague, a Christian can be drawn to take up nursing or hunger relief work. Or again, after a deprived childhood, persons who gain an education may return to their community to work for the welfare of their people. Individuals go back to the slum neighborhood or to the poverty stricken rural region to establish schools, community organizations or drug abuse programs.

Other people choose to dedicate their future working lives to alleviating or eradicating the circumstances that brought tragic suffering to their families, as in drunk driving deaths, debilitating diseases, drug epidemics or mental illnesses. Disciples are called to healing work that imitates Christ when they alleviate and prevent sufferings they have seen firsthand.

At the other extreme are those Christians who find their vocations from the many blessings and good fortune bestowed on them. Individuals who possess talent and intellect and are also born into families that possess wealth, culture and social connections can choose work that takes advantage of their unique privileges. Florence Nightingale comes to mind as an example of a talented, wealthy young woman who was inspired to use her resources and family connections to revolutionize nursing and nineteenth-century England's healthcare. Many saintly founders of religious orders, political movements, scholars, musicians and artists have made use of their positive head starts in finding their life's work. "For this I was born," could be their refrain, echoing the words of Christ.

It is no accident that so many American women achievers who have first broken the glass ceilings in different fields, were able to succeed in nontraditional fields of work partly because they came from families where their fathers (and often their mothers) encouraged them to follow in the family profession or line of work. The present Speaker of the House of Representatives, Nancy Pelosi, not only has a supportive husband who has helped raise their four children, but also had a father who was a prominent politician when she was growing up in Baltimore. Moreover, she attended Trinity College, a Catholic women's school, in Washington, D.C., in an era when the Catholic feminist movement was flowering and encouraging women's accomplishments. Religious orders of nuns always provided models of feminine leadership and achievement, but the big change in Catholic culture came when married women's careers were encouraged and promoted.

In the present era of new opportunities and new decisions, Christian women can pray to the Holy Spirit for the gifts of wisdom, counsel and prudence—along with the courage to follow their vision in the face of inner and outer opposition. Over the years every new work or goal I ever achieved began with a sudden image or aspiration that sprang into my mind, often inspired by an encounter with an admired woman. "Oh how I'd love to be like her," I'd think. "But," I would then object, "I could never do that—have a big family, write a book, go to graduate school, give a public talk, teach or do psychotherapy." Slowly, however, after much reflection and prayer overcame my self-doubt, it turned out that, "Yes, I could do that." If I shaped the ambition into a focused plan and took it step by step, things got accomplished. Preserving my focus and perseverance were rewarded. So it may have taken twenty-five years to get the necessary graduate degrees, but there was plenty of time left for good work. Women's patterns of career development may differ today when life extension and good health have increased.

Today too an important source of insight and encouragement can be found in ongoing psychological research on the role of work in human lives. The essential nature of work and its appropriate function in human flourishing is still emerging; Christians are not the only ones upholding the value of work in our world.

Psychological and Experiential Perspectives on Women's Work

What defines work? Wives and mothers work in the home as well as in the paid and unpaid workforce. Yet the word *work* as in, "working mother" is most often used to refer to labor that is done for money and takes place in offices and institutions. These definitions are still slippery in this society since women also earn money by working at home. Women who no longer live on farms or share in the family agricultural economy may not sell eggs or butter, but they can still earn income at home in other ways. They may care for other children along with their own or fulfill paid assignments of typing, editing, writing, keeping books, sewing or other work. The Internet and direct marketing is producing more opportunities for working at home at the same time it is changing other patterns of work.

Women also do volunteer or unpaid work at home, as well as volunteer in outside settings. Volunteer work may be informal and ad hoc, or highly organized and demanding. American women can be found running libraries, churches, schools, political and civic organizations, charity organizations, self-help groups, ambulance teams, soccer leagues, scout troops and art programs among other community work. Without women's hours of volunteering, civil society would grind to a halt. But what defines work, whether paid or unpaid? How is it different from play?

Work involves sustained effort that is directed toward a designated goal which includes some constraints, usually of a time limit for its completion. Play, by contrast, may include sustained effort as in a game of tennis, but it is freely pursued for pleasure alone and only as long as it is enjoyable. Work is work because it possesses some necessary demand with some goal or finish line that can mark its completion. Paid work includes in its requirements a defined pay scale as well as a time schedule for some exchange of money for service.

Family and domestic unpaid work is surely work but it can have a more fluid time line and set of constraints. Housework can include a series of overlapping tasks such as doing the dishes, the laundry, the food shopping and cooking, paying the bills, reconciling the checks, and a hundred other tasks required in running a household which readers will be able to enumerate. Recently attention has been directed to the amount of effort it takes in order to be able to engage in formal periods designated as "work." This hidden or unnoticed work has been called "shadow work" and consists of the time spent commuting, shopping and preparing work clothes or juggling and arranging family schedules in order to get to work. Arranging and supervising childcare is a major job for working mothers. Shadow work takes energy although it tends to be unnoticed.

Planning and preparing for employment is work. High level volunteer work also may include organizing and supervising schedules, such as in running a church bazaar, chairing PTA meetings, teaching Sunday school or recruiting and supervising hospital volunteers. Basically work consists of any focused effort that fulfills some commitment under constraints of time and place—whether paid or not. The constraints and necessity have meant that work has been seen as mainly negative or as a punishment. While excessive work can be punitive and slaves, serfs and oppressed people can be worked to death, work that is not destructively consuming has its positive effects for human beings.

Meeting the challenges that work presents can be deeply satisfying and rewarding to human beings. Work provides happiness just as leisure or contemplation does. The constraints of a task give a focus to attention and induce concentration. Satisfying work presents engagement and a challenge to competence and the exercise of intelligence. When a goal is met amidst constraints a sense of accomplishment emerges. This drive to meet and complete a challenge has been called *self-efficacy*, and considered to be an innate motivating drive in human beings, beginning in early childhood. The basic emotions of interest and curiosity initiate exploration which generate focused efforts for a goal.

As a child matures, the ability to concentrate, persevere and control her efforts will obtain desired goals. Competence and character grow as attention can be focused and sustained, despite distractions or desires for pleasure. Freud defined mental health as having the ability to love and work, and both require the ability to sustain attentive self-giving effort outside the self. Indeed, in all human societies being able to fulfill a skill with competence gives status and self-respect. To be a good hunter, gatherer, medicine woman or their modern equivalents, gives rewards and a sense of self-worth. Work is an essential good of life.

Today psychologists turning to the study of positive and optimum experiences have identified an intensely satisfying kind of work activity called *flow*. The name is given to the activity because the process carries a person along toward the goal without conscious effort or struggle. Flow occurs when attention is engaged in a task that is neither too easy nor too hard for the worker. Too easy and the work becomes repetitious, tedious and excruciatingly boring; too difficult, and a person becomes frustrated, anxiously self-conscious and overwhelmed. Like little bear's porridge, flow activities are just right.

In flow, a person's interests and abilities are perfectly matched to the challenge of the task. A highly-focused, absorbed person loses track of time and those intrusive distractions that produce internal self-criticism and self-doubt. Attention is directed outward as dynamic efforts are required to respond to the ongoing series of challenges that moves toward the goal. While intensely absorbed in the task, a person is transported beyond the self. Yet afterward, flow experiences produce a sense of enhanced self-efficacy and self-renewal. Such work can produce its own exhilarating high. When a woman says "I love my work, and I would do it even if they didn't pay me," she is describing a positive human experience.

Granted, flow experiences arise while engaging in music, dancing, painting, running, mountain climbing and having sexual intercourse. Intensely stimulating conversation, worship or group celebrations can also engender flow. Mystics report that in joyful contemplative prayer they lose track of time and self-consciousness. Working intensely in a flow state for a good goal can produce a joyful sense of transported self expansion. Perhaps this is what Jesus is referring to when he tells his disciples to take his yoke upon them, because it is light. Jesus' words that he who loses his soul for the Lord's sake will find it also describe the paradox that giving is a form of receiving. The humility of the self-forgetful worker is liberating and rewarding.

On a more prosaic level, women and men reap positive secondary rewards from work, even beyond earning money to provide for their own and their family's needs. Women can appreciate the perks of work that can bring comrades, colleagues and teammates. To participate in a structured, larger world beyond the household broadens perspectives. Solidarity with other workers who are not your family members can give experiences of cooperative effort aimed at communal and civic goals. Isolated women at home can welcome going out to conduct business. In an earlier time women washing clothes together in a stream, or gathering roots automatically had access to companionship and communal work. Women, like all human adults, need the primary and secondary fulfillments of good work.

In a developed technological society many educated women will have prepared themselves over many years of training to be competent in highly demanding, absorbing work that produces flow experiences for them. While other kinds of work at home and with their families can be equally valued by these women, it will not allow them to use their specialized talents and capacities. Withdrawal from this specialized work may create a kind of misery. Such women will need to find settings in which to perform the work they need for their well being. I for instance always wilt and become unhappy when I cannot study or write. Nothing can be more emotionally and personally challenging and satisfying than caring for babies and children, but it does not engage highly abstract problem solving challenges on which I thrive.

When women are deprived of satisfying work that is matched to their capacities and competence, they are deprived of experiences of self-efficacy and absorbing flow states. Idle, unchallenged and indolent, women (or men) easily become apathetic and unhappy, even if it is not true that the devil finds work for idle hands. It isn't only about having one's own money or independent status, but underemployment of personal talents and capabilities leads to frustration. How sad that so many middle-class women in the past were barred by their gentility from either the vigorous housework which was relegated to servants, or the rigorous education and opportunity to work in the public sphere. Their status as ladies imprisoned them on their protected pedestals.

Whatever the era, underemployed women can be reduced to trivial pursuits and dissipation, if not depression or drug abuse. But recognizing the value and psychological necessity of having good work does not resolve the specific issue of how to find and pursue it. Difficult questions remain of how women can combine work and family life. This is the crux of the debate once more being initiated.

A Feminist Argument for Going to Work and Staying There

Feisty pro-career feminist arguments currently insist that *every* woman should get to work and *stay* there. Work is defined as a career or sustained paid employment outside of the home, with only the briefest interruption for childbearing and maternity leave. Dropping out of the work force, goes this admonition, will make a woman vulnerable to a host of penalties and financial disasters. If an unemployed wife is abandoned, divorced or widowed she and her children will face impoverishment. When a woman retains her independent income she can provide support for herself and her children. She can ensure her children's education and her own financial security in old age.

Moreover, the argument goes, married women who do not earn money will lose power within a marriage where a highly paid husband earns all of the family money. The social realities of male privilege and cultural gender assumptions will conspire with economics to nudge non-working wives into subordinate roles. Without equal earning power women will not have equal decisionmaking power. And if a woman needs to leave her marriage she will not find it easy to do so. Without access to continuing paid employment, a woman will be trapped in inequality.

Another negative consequence predicted for women who drop out of the workforce is their difficulty of reentry when middle-aged. If women wait to return to work until their children are grown, they will have lost their place in the career ladder and will never make up the loss. They will not be able to reenter at a career level where they can have challenging and well paid work. The social system and the world of work remains stacked against women, especially older women, without current skills. Recognizing the social realities, women are enjoined to take off their rose-colored glasses and persevere in their employment and careers. They must resist all temptations to quit in order to take care of their families.

CREATING NEW LIFE, NURTURING FAMILIES

This insistent pro-career message can even go so far as to advise women not to have more than one child. With two or more children, a move to the suburbs becomes likely which will make it more difficult to commute to the workplace. Living in the suburbs and having more than one child will increase the domestic pressures on women to fall into traditional gender roles and give up demanding work. Even with only one child, the pro-career argument claims, women who work will have to fight off the cultural pressure for wives to assume all the responsibility for the household as well as for the current hyper-parenting norms that consume women's energy and time.

In affluent competitive families that can afford to hire help, child-rearing standards and schedules can become so excessive that mothers can still spend their days scheduling appointments, supervising the hired help and supporting school and extracurricular activities. In addition, planning and carrying out elaborate holiday celebrations, birthday parties and family vacations and other luxuries can become demanding tasks.

The stay-at-work message to women, forcefully asserts that they must make active efforts not to be sucked into a downward domestic spiral that ends in secondhand status and citizenship. When financial and social underachievement is an acceptable norm for educated and talented women, they will no longer be taken seriously in the public and civic sphere. Professional achievement and money are what count in exercising influence. It is far better for a woman to have an equal, two-career, one-child family, no matter how many sacrifices it takes to stay working during the early years of family life.

Realistically planning ahead, young women should begin in their college years not to shirk the harder mathematical, statistical and scientific courses which will lead to more remunerative mainline jobs. They should not enter feminine fields with lower status and less pay. Mommy track arrangements and part-time work should be avoided. Working women should be told to aim for the top in their field and take pains to stay in the mainstream where they have the greatest access to power and earn higher salaries. Like men, women should discipline themselves to work hard and stay the course which will lead to the highest career success. After all, when a woman's children are grown, a woman who has invested in her career will still have satisfying work. She can still enjoy her professional colleagues and have her talents engaged, along with financial security.

The Choice to Stay Home

While an assertive pro-career perspective on women's work contains a certain truth, it is not the whole truth. Christians can agree with the value conferred on seeking challenging work and on the discipline it takes to persevere and achieve success. The ability to set priorities, simplify life and preserve focus is admirable. But there are also serious inadequacies in a message to women that they should focus primarily on obtaining financial reward, high status and security. Many critical voices contend that it is not enough to achieve success in a high paying, highly demanding career to have a good life. Achieving a high income and gaining professional status does not automatically bring happiness or even guarantee enlivening flow experiences—as the lives of many successful men demonstrate. Moral, aesthetic, social and spiritual values also must be satisfied for a good life.

It is also not true that income and professional achievement are the main sources of power and influence in our society. In the family or in the community social influence arises from personally committed investments of time and emotion in interpersonal relationships with others. Women who choose to give up their outside work, either permanently or temporarily, and focus their working efforts within the family and community, can have good and worthy lives that bring them and others the highest levels of happiness. The growing number of highly educated young women who drop out of careers do so for personal as well as altruistic reasons.

Many women have not warmed to the competitive aggressive machismo culture of many corporations, professions and academic settings. If the long term purpose of a business or profession is to make more money for rich people, or to achieve some other socially suspect goal, many women will not be motivated to persevere in the system. For instance, it might be stimulating and highly remunerative to work every day with bright colleagues marketing cigarettes but not be satisfying to a woman's ultimate moral values. The moral meaning of work can be more important than the process, when a woman has freedom of choice. Money and financial security do not trump all other considerations.

More troubling yet are those drastic pro-career demands that childbearing be limited to one child for the sake of continuing employment. This can seem too great a price to pay when assessing what is most valuable in human life. It can also be a mistaken view of what gives a woman influence and happiness in the long run. Having an unfashionably large number of children, for instance, brings women social power and rewarding emotional connections that money cannot buy. Investment in the next generation and in the local community becomes concrete in the rearing of children—and grandchildren. The satisfactions of extended families can become particularly valuable and joyful for older women who would otherwise be retired.

Women who stay home and trust in their husband's faithfulness and commitment as the family provider, do not appear naïve if their marriages are founded on mutual trust and mutual religious commitments. Should a woman's decisions be dominated by risk-aversive calculations of betrayal and disaster? If a marital or family breakdown does occur and a woman finds herself alone, what can equal the support of a loving extended family and strong caring community? The bonds which buoy up women in misfortune are built up during the years invested in family, friends, church membership and neighborhood connections. Colleagues at work often exist as quasi-competitors and tend to come and go. They rarely can give the unconditional emotional support that irreversibly related families and local communities do. Friendships at work easily fade because of transfers and retirements. Family ties abide.

Women do not drop out from work and careers only to overparent or micromanage their children's highly programmed lives. Many women stop outside work when their children are young because of the damaging stress of combining family and work. The tension and scarcity of time for communication and restorative leisure becomes destructive. The pressures of managing conflicting demands of two high-pressured careers with less than ideal childcare arrangements becomes its own form of servitude. Why have two parents on exhausting career treadmills if one parent is well paid enough to support the household?

Unfortunately for families today, the forty-hour work weeks of yesteryear have now increased to sixty- or seventy-hour schedules. Frequent business travel to different cities or countries is routine. In the grind of career requirements, Americans can find themselves sacrificing or scanting family time, friendship, leisure, culture, hospitality and commitments to church, charity work and civic activities. Who has the time to volunteer in a political campaign or take part in a protest movement for peace or justice? There is little energy left after long exhausting work days to be able to organize musical groups, Bible study classes or serve in soup kitchens. Ill relatives and elderly neighbors get less visiting or assistance than they should.

Mothers of autistic, developmentally disabled or mentally ill children will confront a society that does even less for them than other families. Few parents have access to excellent affordable daycare or specialized programs for those with special needs. Women with impaired children may have to become their children's fulltime caretakers and advocates in unresponsive social circumstances. Women volunteers may take on fulltime roles in reforming the community's systems for impaired children. They work in unpaid efforts to help the welfare of others as well as their own children.

In the end many women with the financial resources to do so can decide that their lives and that of their children will be better in every way if they stay at home, either temporarily or permanently. As one young working woman said, "I see that I have been successfully 'managing' my children, but not really having the time to be present with them." It is one thing to discipline one's self to persevere in a demanding career, and another thing to deprive one's children and family of a full life. The years of childhood go by very fast and the years spent in creating a strong family and home life are irreplaceable.

Moreover, despite the dire warnings of the pro-career position, women today may have hopes of successfully reentering the workforce after their children are older. The values and satisfactions of highly challenging work may not be given up for good as a penalty for stopping out. Flexible new patterns of work and careers have been emerging in a fluid society influenced by the Internet. Many modern women manage to compose a life that incorporates different marital and family contingencies. New interests also develop and stimulate the acquisition of new skills leading to different work opportunities than they might have chosen earlier. Fortunately, America is the land of second acts and second careers and this openness can help middle-aged women who desire to reenter the work world.

Deciding Priorities

First and foremost, parental responsibility for one's children is a basic moral obligation. Another fundamental ethical command for all those entrusted with the health and welfare of others is that they should "do no harm." In the case of parents it seems that their altruism is an innate universal human trait that has been selected by genetic and cultural evolution. Christianity affirms this natural predisposition by asserting that the well being of children should have priority over the adults in a family, by virtue of parental obligation and because children are the most vulnerable members of the human family. The duty to put children's needs first is also supported by the fact that children go through critical periods of development in which neglect can impair their future lives. Children are resilient but it is not clear how much harm can be undone. A child's need for physical and emotional care are not separate and crucial capacities for their future functioning depend upon loving, sensitive nurturing.

Attentive loving care in a specific period may influence a child's intelligence, language ability, emotional responsiveness, identity and basic trust toward the world. Many theorists also consider that religious experiences of the sacred arise from the first interpersonal relationship with the mothering one. Given these considerations, a Christian's acceptance of the command to love others as God loves us, would mean that parents should make personal sacrifices for a child—both to prevent harm and to ensure future flourishing. A faithful mother puts her dependent child's well being first, and if and when it is necessary she will sacrifice her own needs.

Millions of mothers have in the past and are in the present sacrificing themselves for their children's welfare. Impoverished women have no other choice for their children's survival than to toil in exploitative oppressive jobs. Immigrants, migrant workers, displaced refugees and others endure exhausting low-paying jobs that are a form of wage slavery. Women labor for their families' survival in the present but also in hope that their children may gain the education and skills they need to procure better work and a better life. Generations of poor women and men have sacrificed themselves in hopes of a better future for the next generation. Mothers and fathers have worked several shifts or endured years of crushing labor in order to make their dreams for their children come true.

The dream can become nearer for many fortunate women today. They can achieve the fulfillment of good work and good family lives that their foremothers could only imagine. The satisfactions of stimulating work in a career can be achieved by many women while they also have a family life with well-nurtured flourishing children. Women can have positive flow experiences in well-paid work when their individual talents, education and skills match their opportunities for work that needs doing. With enough income such a working mother may be able to hire the competent help she and her children need. Good daycare may be available. Increasingly, many institutions are striving to keep their competent women workers by providing daycare at work, and instituting family-friendly policies.

Another helpful component of the dream for working women is the presence of grandparents and extended family support with childcare. Having relatives and community to call upon is a priceless resource for all mothers, but this is particularly true for working women. Grandmothers and grandfathers are the most invested caretakers because they are serving their bonds of kinship as well as providing conscientious childcare.

The most utopian circumstance for working women will be to have a husband who is committed to an equal and cooperative marriage and family life. A supportive husband shares as an equal co-parent and an equal worker in the household. A demanding two-career family can be possible when both spouses share equally in building the family and both of their careers. In some new family arrangements, wives and husbands may take turns in fulfilling the education requirements for their careers; they may consider both spouses' professional opportunities to be equal. The husband's education and professional goals are not always put first at the expense of the wife's. The ideal husband and father is committed to his family and his work, and takes his share in all of the maintenance work of a home. In fact men who temporarily stay home as househusbands are no longer regularly stigmatized. This change reflects the relationship between the genders in America as well as an understanding that childcare and homemaking are valuable.

In just and loving families who live the Christian ideal, everyone's needs count, but those who are more vulnerable at the moment are given greater priority. Dependent children come first, but a woman's calling to engage in absorbing, highly demanding work is as valued and accommodated as that of men has traditionally been. In a loving and just society the discipline, focus and sacrifices necessary for a woman to pursue work that challenges her, will be encouraged and supported. Christians do not aspire to live by selfish calculations of financial risks and rewards, but to seek fulfilling work as their way to serve God's creation. Families of faith know they should be ready to sacrifice financial rewards and career status for the sake of nurturing their children, but they can aspire toward the ideal of having women and men pursue work that fulfills them.

Children who are lovingly nurtured and provided for materially can benefit from their parents' commitment to equality, justice and commitments to good work. These families can feel that they have had the best of lives for all concerned. In the same way, children whose mothers and fathers had to give up their work satisfaction for the family's sake will honor their parents' altruism. When circumstances, social limitations and human fallibility frustrate the fulfillment of family members, sadness over failures also can be faced honestly.

Failure in work and family life is as much a part of the human condition as success. Uncontrollable events can interact with personal circumstances so that waste and sorrow mar lives. Christian women must be prepared to mourn and understand the suffering and losses that come to everyone. But is there a unique Christian approach to failure and suffering? The next chapter will focus on these questions of travail and how suffering is related to Christian promises of joy.

Food for Thought

1. Have you taken your gifts and talents for work seriously enough? What aspirations and goals have you sought and obtained in different kinds of work?
2. What flow experiences have you had? What kinds of rewards have you received from different work experiences?

3. What conflicts and difficulties have you experienced between your different commitments to family and to work? How did you resolve them or compose your life?

PRAYER

Invocation:
God Our Creator,
  Be with us as we work.
God Our Creator,
  Inspire us for work that meets the needs of others.
God Our Creator,
  Make us steadfast in seeking good work.

Scripture: 1 Corinthians 15:58

Response:
Let us place ourselves in God's presence and reflect on all the choices of work we have made in the past, and consider how we made them. Help us to appreciate all that we do in caring for our families, as well as to affirm all of the volunteer labor and paid work we have done beyond our homes.

Let us recall mistaken choices and failures in our working lives. Help us to know in our hearts that you accept our failures and always forgive us. We offer you the disappointments or times of drudgery we have endured.

Let us now dream boldly of what work we can aspire to in our future lives. Help us to discern our potential for the work God is calling us to do.

Prayer:
Christ who is working to renew our creation, be with us. As we work, in, with and through your power let us bear good fruit. Bring to completion all of our efforts to build families and communities that will give you glory and bring God's kingdom to earth. Keep us steadfast in

our labor and inspire our hope for the coming of God's kingdom. Let us remember that nothing good we do is wasted and that all will be well. Amen.

CHAPTER SEVEN

SUFFERING, JOY AND TRANSFORMATION

Suffering and joy are the most intense emotions that mark a wife and mother's life. Shouldn't Christians on their journey to God be prepared to undergo suffering with courage and fully celebrate joy? The great promise has been given that Christ's disciples will be given wisdom of the Holy Spirit, and be enabled to become like Christ Jesus, the firstborn of many brothers and sisters in God's new family. As Daniel Keating states in *Deification and Graces,* "The Son of God became the Son of Man, so that the sons and daughters of men might become the sons and daughters of God."[2] Christ's suffering, death and resurrection liberates human beings from death and despair and transforms them with joy.

Our human sufferings, like our work, can be joined to Christ's work of bringing the new creation to birth. As Saint Paul says, "We know that the whole creation has been groaning in labor pains until now; and not only the creation, but we ourselves, who have the first fruits of the Spirit, groan inwardly while we wait for adoption, the redemption of our bodies" (Romans 8:22–23). The eager longing of creation has been joyfully fulfilled in Christ's resurrection and is now coming to fruition. Our human joys are not illusory self-deceptions but real manifestations of God's love for the world. Joy is a fruit of the Holy Spirit, a luminous manifestation of God's real presence. Christians are called to live in joyful hope. With the reception of the gifts of love and joy, the faithful are strengthened to bear all burdens patiently. Day by day, minute by minute, Christians seek to grow up into Christ. Disciples labor to become more completely conformed to his mind and heart. The goal is to be another Christ.

The command to love God and neighbor as Christ does must be carried out in thought, word and deed. Slowly and gradually the new seed flowers and bears fruit. The infant's imperial self that wants what it wants when it wants it, has to give way and open up to the transformed human being. The "me and mine" that is perpetually insecure, afraid, envious and grasping has to open up to God's light and love. This transforming process, like that of the groaning creation, includes birth pangs. Each Christian's inner struggle toward the light is inevitably resisted by the forces of inertia in the world. As Christians seek to grow in love they meet obstacles within and outside themselves. In an evolving incomplete disordered world disciples have to take up their cross for Christ's sake. This means acting, persisting, keeping the hand to the plow and not turning back from love's work.

Jesus comes to serve his brothers and sisters and so must those who would be called his friends and followers. Taking up and bearing the cross with Jesus can bring suffering and opposition, but at the same time Christ's disciples are promised a joy that no one can take from them. Yet how can this be true? Living an abundant life of joy is promised here and now, not only in a future life in God's kingdom. The puzzle turns on how the intense and contradictory experiences of joy and suffering can be put together. One apt image used by both Jesus and by Saint Paul is that of a woman in childbirth. Giving birth brings labor and pain but also the joy of creating new life. The transforming growing process of individuals and the creation appear bound up in experiences of intense joy and acute suffering. Christians do well to ponder on these things.

Thinking About Suffering

We may know suffering when we meet it, but defining and understanding the different kinds and causes of suffering is not simple. For an experience to count as suffering it has to be intense and severely, seriously aversive for me. It must be beyond annoyance or irritation. In suffering I desperately, obsessively desire things to be different or undone, but I cannot make it go away. The excruciating physical or psychological distress continues outside of my control. I cannot stop the pain, cure the disease or reverse my losses. The coming of death is the ultimate suffering we face. I cannot have my dead child back alive or my deceased father and mother return. Other irreversible conditions bring pain. We suffer when our physical, emotional or social integrity and wholeness as a person is seriously assaulted by forces beyond our control. A rejection or betrayal by a lover, husband, child or friend can be as excruciatingly painful as physical injury.

Suffering also comes from being deprived, or by the absence of something. Deprivations can cause suffering, beginning with food and shelter and moving on to human social needs. All sorts of refusals and rejections can cause severe distress. Educational, employment and civic opportunities can be unjustly denied to a person because of their race, gender, age, sexual orientation or class. Blacks and women have suffered in the very recent past from denials of opportunities for higher schooling, good jobs and full civic equality. Habitual demeaning prejudice inflicted in contemptuous and insulting language and gesture can cause distress. When your dignity and equality is rejected it becomes clear that for human beings, "sticks and stones may break my bones but names will *always* hurt me." To be shunned and shut out from the group may be excruciating for hyper-social beings.

Persons are victimized by suffering because their pain is involuntarily imposed upon them. Victims are innocent of causing either the accidental events or the cruel action of more powerful others. More complicated cases of suffering also exist. Often the victim and victimizer are one and the assault on self's integrity comes from within. Inner conflict and misery can arise from personal flaws or willful resistance to the acknowledged good action. Emotional responses such as rage, envy, jealousy or injured pride can be severely distressing, albeit self-originated. Agonies of guilt, shame, remorse and regret can also arise from an agent's past actions and attitudes. Complex emotional states of misery severely afflict persons, arising partly from their own actions but also at times from out of control addictions of various kinds.

Those who suffer may sometimes be suffering the painful consequences of slavery to habits that may have begun as freely chosen selfish acts. Addicted persons cling to their self-induced misery. In other situations, a freely chosen misdeed can interact with chance events and magnify the distressing consequences for everyone involved, including the innocent, as when a mother leaves her child alone to run to the store and there is a lethal fire.

The assaults of involuntary suffering of every kind can diminish, debilitate, isolate and inflict permanent harm. It is wrongheaded to romanticize and glorify pain and suffering as intrinsically ennobling or uplifting. Too many women who "love too much" have been persuaded that suffering repeated abuse is a proof of true love. Persons can be broken, impaired and afflicted by suffering. They can be stunted and numbed or too traumatized to recover, as with many survivors of state inflicted torture. Victims of suffering and abuse are not automatically wiser or morally better.

By itself, suffering implies only two necessary conclusions. One, people cannot control it, and two, *all* human beings are vulnerable. These bare truths may serve to harden a survivor who can respond with a vow to never again risk losing control or giving up power over others. The tough survivor refuses to identify with the weak or vulnerable. Worse still, bitter survivors may seek revenge on life and turn upon those who are weaker than themselves. Victims can become victimizers. The abused child becomes a bully, the tortured prisoner becomes a terrorist. Cycles of pain and violence are perpetuated. But there is another response to human suffering, and a different kind of suffering.

Another Kind of Response

The suffering that leads to wisdom will do so by refusing to harden one's heart. Openness and empathy are chosen instead of closed defensiveness or aggression. Empathy, as we have discussed here earlier, is that innate, intuitive and instantaneous subjective participation in another person's response. As newly discovered mirror neuron systems in the brain indicate, human beings automatically produce, or mirror, the response that they observe in another. The mirrored responses produce the same feelings in a shared consciousness. This is why emotions are contagious so that I feel what you feel. When I see you smile, I smile, when I see you suffer and weep, I suffer too.

But this intuitive automatic human response can be suppressed, or turned off voluntarily, at least by normal adults. It is possible for people to turn away, to quickly shut down feelings of empathy. This ability to adopt a heart of stone, to distance oneself and deaden empathy can help explain torturers and war criminals; it can also help to explain our own insensitive behavior on our worst days.

To accept or stay with the feeling of empathy means that we accept and share others' suffering. Opening the self to the other is the response of a heart of flesh; empathy sustained motivates altruistic action. Altruistic impulses to alleviate suffering are as much a part of our evolved human nature as the selfish drive to survive through aggression. Even small children can sense another's pain and try to offer comfort with a toy or favorite blanket. It appears from new infant studies and findings from the evolutionary history of humans, that human possession of innate responses of empathy produces innate moral motivations and intuitions.

Empathy that is sustained and developed with intelligent attention to the other's needs in the situation producees sympathy and effective remedial actions. Human powers of rationality when motivated by empathy are employed to relieve suffering and prevent it in the future. Human progress, as in the case of medicine, has consisted of ingenuity driven by desires to relieve and eradicate human suffering. A wife and mother's desire to nurture, protect and alleviate her children's suffering is an innate and universal motivating response.

It is also the case that the capacity of empathy increases vicarious suffering in the world. Many men and women may suffer more with those they love than they do in any direct assaults on themselves. Good health and good fortune can protect an adult in a developed civilized country from much of the world's external miseries. And many mature, morally socialized men and women also have grown beyond the rebelliousness that produces chaotic, self-induced suffering. Infantile, selfish personalities tend to lurch from disaster to disaster. By contrast, normal maturing processes can achieve a degree of emotional intelligence and adequate self-governance. Every one will sin, but many adults overcome bouts of neurotic suffering and avoid dangers from the environment.

But empathetic suffering with the sufferings of others will exist in the lives of all those who love. A mother will suffer in empathy with her son or daughter's pain and distress no matter how old the child. A woman's own well being cannot prevent her family's suffering. It is impossible to undo a child's genetic impairment, accidental injury, serious illness or sudden death. Grown children suffer from personality flaws, addictions, mental illness, career failures, divorces, moral lapses and tragic situations with their own children. Spouses have heart attacks, older parents become forgetful or fragile, adult children can be arrested, maimed or killed in a war or street violence. Women will mourn; Rachel can be heard weeping for her children. Surely, the traditional devotion to Mary grieving at the foot of the cross witnesses to the prevailing reality in life of empathetic pain.

What mother, holding her child suffering from some dreadful disease or life threatening accidental disaster, has not felt a sword pass through her heart? A suffering mother can yearn to bear the pain in her child's stead. These moments give human beings the merest glimpse of God's loving empathy with us and the force of the Divine desire to rescue humankind from death, pain and destruction. Christ's suffering with us and for us can become more vividly imagined as we grieve with and for others. For our sake, Christ the sinless one, directly endured calumny, rejection, betrayal, persecution, humiliation, violent assault and an excruciating torturous execution.

Christ also suffered as he lamented for all his people who would reject his words and persist in their self-destructive path. His empathy extended to his enemies and sinners, as well as to victims of disease, oppression and death. God's love and empathy does not set moral conditions. Human empathy also can be felt for those who are too morally deformed to recognize their own depraved grotesqueness. A faith-filled person can feel distress over another person's absence of moral guilt and shame. To see others with hardened hearts and stunted consciences provokes pain, however contented and heedless they may be of their state.

Involuntary suffering arouses empathy for victims, but so can blameworthy self-induced conditions. A mother suffers in the punishment meted out to her erring child, however just or deserved it may be. The father of the prodigal son did not stop loving and sorrowing over the sins of his wastrel son. Empathy and sorrow can be felt for the guilty and morally debased as well as for the innocent. Indignation and anger give way to vicarious shame and depression that fellow human beings can sink so low.

So too, the absence or lack of self-awareness in those who innocently suffer dementia or mental impairment induces sadness. Their diminished state may protect them from subjective suffering, but loving caretakers can still feel pain for their plight. Those who spend time in an Alzheimer's facility, as I do visiting my frail and sweetly confused ninety-five-year-old stepmother, can mourn the loss of sense and functioning ability. The person is beloved of God and family, and possesses an inalienable moral dignity—that shines through the fog—but sorrow over loss still prevails.

Fortunately, empathetic suffering is the one form of suffering that does not tend to isolate, narrow, constrict or diminish the sufferer. Rather, a compassionate heart is enlarged, deepened and expanded in consciousness despite sorrow. In empathy a person reaches out and unites with the other. Forgiveness of all injuries comes easily. In a word, empathy and love suffer with the other, and in so doing motivate self-giving acts of mercy, reconciliation and healing.

God, who is all good and supreme in empathy, never sends suffering or evil to humankind. God in Christ wills and works for all of creation's joy and flourishing. Only the freedom and openness of the evolving universe makes it possible for independent free beings to reject God, suppress empathy and do evil. The freedom necessary to grow up and become God's friends also allows room for rebellion, evil and sin. Only free human beings who can say yes or no to love could undertake the privileged task of cocreating God's kingdom of love.

With their gifts of freedom and rationality, Christians are called to develop the world, heal it and celebrate the love that makes it possible. If selfishness makes people reject empathy and run away from any and all suffering, then they will not be able to fulfill a commitment to love and work. Being unwilling to lose their lives, they will not find them.

Joy Amid Suffering?

Is there then nothing but pain and suffering in the Christian disciple's life? First there is the inner and external struggle to be born anew and to renew the world. Human inertia and resistance to the new is strong. Second, Christians can suffer persecution directed at them, as well as be caught in the power of the oppressive social sin that deforms the world. Domineering structures of greed exploit and grind people down. Thirdly, natural disorders of death and disease take their toll. Finally, individuals will be vulnerable to sinful acts of individual cruelty.

But Christ promises joy and peace as he comes to liberate and save humankind from death and suffering. Jesus makes it clear that he cherishes the good and well being of each individual that lives. Human losses and suffering are never countenanced but reversed, even dangerous storms are quieted and food and wine provided for the needy. Life is to be valued and not thrown away. Jesus counsels his disciples to be "wise as serpents and innocent as doves" (Matthew 10:16). Good decision-making or the virtue of prudence is often held up for praise in the Gospels. Reading the signs of the times, disciples are told to flee to the hills to avoid the coming destruction of Jerusalem. Jesus himself outwits his enemies, faces down a lynch mob, eludes the temple police and avoids arrest until his chosen moment arrives. Praying in the Garden of Gethsemane he groans over the dreadful suffering and death he is to endure. When arrested he saves his followers and spares his captors.

Taking up the cross for Jesus' sake is not a glorification of the value of suffering or the life of a victim. Rather, it is only necessary suffering incurred in loving efforts to end suffering that is commended. The loving intent of Christians is to heal all wounds. Christ the great physician offers his remedy. Forgiveness of sins can heal self-inflicted sufferings from guilt and shame. Christ's loving attentiveness to the inestimable worth of each human being cures self-loathing. Liberations from death and the offer of life as God's friends and coworkers gives meaning and purpose to life. Altruistic suffering that is necessary for loving mercy may be painful but it will expand and enlarge the self in communion with God.

Persons can identify with the poor, the ill, the oppressed and the deprived because the capacity of empathy allows them to imagine the misery of others and feel as they would feel. Today, psychology and neuroscience also can help explain to us how our unique human brain power allows humans to project themselves into the future and imagine different circumstances than the present. This capacity for foresight may be the most unique of all human capacities. Admittedly, it can bring anxiety and fear of our future death, but it can also inspire hope and effective work to overcome present sufferings. The will to help others is strengthened by the capacity to imagine and carry through change for the better. Justice, mercy and healing can become effective as persons determine to make new things happen. "Behold I make all things new," says the Lord.

Over and over Christ preached God's love and saving power to rescue and save those who are suffering. God's kingdom is come, the bread is rising. Yes, the disordered world can resist change and its own salvation, but death and stubborn suffering will not have the last word. The resurrection of Jesus proves that death cannot hold Christ. By uniting with Jesus the Son of Man, disciples can be raised to eternal life. Christian disciples can be comforted and strengthened in their suffering by their trust in the promises of God. Every tear will be wiped away and there will be no more mourning and weeping when God is all in all.

Hope for future rescue lifts the spirits in any siege or battle. For that matter, a woman in childbirth endures through hope. The sufferings of the present time can be known as the birth pangs of the new creation. Christians whose suffering cannot be alleviated or whose merciful efforts to love others meet failure can take heart in the fact that their intractable suffering and failure is not meaningless. Every moment of every event, no matter how painful, futile and absurd, can be offered in love to God and participate in the birth process begun on the cross. Successes and victories are delightful offerings, but the faithful also know that failure, frustration, disease, pain and death can be offered to help God's kingdom come.

We need to remind ourselves over and over and forever trust that nothing is wasted, nothing is lost. Whatever is given and received in love finds meaning in God. Christ holds all things together. Love illuminates and encourages the world in joy.

Wellsprings of Joy

Joy is not alien to human nature but is innately present in human beings. From infancy to old age, joy and pleasure powerfully influence all that gets accomplished and experienced by humans. This truth is often ignored because attention is captured by the sharp warning signals of pain and negative emotions. Evolutionary processes have ensured that the negative emotional system in the brain producing pain and suffering are intense and vivid signals. Aversive emotions such as fear and anger must produce quick action and rapid responses for the sake of survival. Pain is the cue that a course correction is called for.

Positive emotions such as joy, happiness, pleasure, playfulness, interest and contentment, by contrast, accompany safety and security. When all is secure we can keep on enjoying what we're doing and explore new things. Continuity, communion and safety release energy for human creativity. Creativity requires a secure haven. Celebration, laughter and joy enliven and quicken all human functioning. Defensiveness and vigilant fear may help ensure survival, but joy and delight make human beings desire to stay alive and beget new life.

Joy and positive emotions of interest become fused in love. Joy is a conscious awareness of delight and pleasure of different kinds. Joy emerges in love of mother and child, in marriage and sex, in music, art, play, work, novelty and glad religious celebrations. In joy, the heart burns and takes flight. Glad moments range from gentle to merry to ecstatic, but they all signal good tidings of great joy. This goodness and happiness gives proof that joy is the ultimate reality. Believers recognize the warming fire as God's presence. Scripture affirms that joy and love are fruits of the Holy Spirit. Where love and joy are there is God. Delight reverberates in consciousness and exuberantly soars upward and outward into pervasive feelings of well being and fulfillment. When desires of mind, body and heart are fulfilled, one's cup runneth over. The Hebrew Psalms give exultant expression to joy in God and creation.

Because of the human capacity for empathy and psychological unity, joy and happiness is as contagious as fear and sadness. Tears beget tears, but laughter induces laughter. Innate experiences of joy, love and beauty infuse human life in normal expectable environments. The mysterious emergence of joy may puzzle those who are resigned to belief in a tragically meaningless universe, but Christians accept the goodness of creation as a sign of their Creator's goodness. The existence of joy and happiness, intelligence and love, is a sign of God's ineffable joy, light and truth. Goodness is acknowledged by traditional philosophers to be self-diffusive. The Divine energy of light, love and joy radiates and pervades reality, magnetically attracting the minds and hearts of humans created in God's image.

Jesus, as God made visible, attracted the crowds as a man filled with love, joy and truth. One traditional title for Jesus is the man of sorrows and aptly names his empathy for his people's suffering and his willingness to suffer in order to liberate, heal and rescue them. However, Jesus also is a man of joy. Jesus rejoices in the Good News he brings of God's salvation and the coming of the kingdom. He comes to break every yoke and free humankind from sin, gloom and oppression. The fire that Jesus is eager to kindle inspires him and he burns with love for God and his brothers and sisters. Christ's intimacy with God produces the compelling goodness, tenderness and healing energy that made the disciples follow him. Jesus ate and drank with all, loved his friends and rejoiced in the God-given beauty of the world and human love. His power and holiness enabled Christ to heal the ill and restore the dead to life.

Early disciples could believe Christ's teachings and promises of joy because of his own life of joy and truth. Jesus is a Hebrew prophet who inspires trust in the victory of God's justice and love. He was able to convey God's joy despite the suffering that exists in a creation groaning toward fulfillment.

Joy in the Midst of Sufferings

Women of faith in our day can also receive glimpses of light and the gift of joy in the midst of the suffering and struggles of daily life. While pain and suffering are real and not an illusion as some thinkers have asserted, joy can be present in the midst of pain. This ability to feel opposite and contradictory emotions, either at the same time or in quick alternations, has been observed in the past, although rarely explained. Today new research on emotions has claimed that it is possible to be happy and sad at the same time because of the way the brain is constructed. Different systems for positive or negative emotions have been evolved and can be activated at the same time. The brain's incredibly complicated organization can operate with different levels active simultaneously.

The ability to have a doubled- or near-simultaneous-contradictory consciousness of positive and negative emotions appears to be a human capacity. Most of us have had the experience of a surge of love and joy during a distressful time, perhaps at a funeral with expressions of love or while being cared for in a painful illness. In research on emotions, widows who were interviewed about their husbands and marriages reported intense sorrow over the death and absence of their mates and at the same time joy in their marital love. Another example might be the experience of a mother whose child has been buried in the rubble of an earthquake and is crying. The child can be extricated through arduous painful effort. As the mother struggles she suffers for and with her crying child, she suffers and bleeds from the painful stones, and at the same time she rejoices that her child is alive and that she can save her.

To feel joy and suffering together it seems necessary to have certain conditions exist. The kind of suffering that can coexist with joy cannot be that of frustrated rage, hostility, envy, lust or wailing and gnashing of teeth. Self-sabotaging destructive willful attitudes of hate or resentment close us in ourselves and block openness to feelings of love, gratitude and joy. Altruistic and innocent suffering in empathy is compatible with joy because love can be present. Love may be the essential condition for experiencing joy amidst suffering. Intense love may induce unquenchable moments of joy. The most extreme witness of this in Christian experience is the example of those martyrs throughout history who have ecstatically proclaimed their joy in God while suffering the torments of torture and death.

Receptiveness to joy and love arise together. Those great mystics who constantly practice the presence of God seem able to rejoice constantly in every state of awareness. They practice the sacrament of the present moment and rejoice always. Their capacities for directing consciousness have developed beyond most of us. But the presence of moments of joy amidst suffering among ordinary people can be seen to follow the same patterns. Loving acts of altruistic sacrifice now can be better understood. The pain is real but so is the joy.

Transformation Through Love and Joy
The Christian claim as voiced by Saint Paul has been that "We know that all things work together for good for those who love God" (Romans 8:28). Now we have some insight into how this can be true. Christians don't necessarily have more good things happen to them, nor do they avoid pain and suffering more than other people. The promise is true because Christians can grow and change from whatever happens to them, and even more consoling, they can trust that their offering of all of their negative and positive experiences will be used in building God's kingdom. All things can have meaning and help transform the individual as well as the whole creation.

The way of love's suffering in Christian life leads to happiness and joy, but the birth process demands discarding and overcoming blameworthy behaviors that block love and gratitude. Uprightness and virtue come from freely enacted repetitions of good choices and refusals to harm others. Habits of virtue are built up, usually quite slowly, so that suffering from self-sabotaging and self-destructiveness are left behind. There are sudden transformations and conversions, like Paul on the road to Damascus, but most personal change is like the seed that sprouts and grows slowly and almost imperceptibly. During a woman's lifelong spiritual transformation she is changed by staying open to empathy and God's love whatever happens.

Persons are moved to efforts and change by desire and magnetic attraction to the good. The great drawing power of God is the wonderful light of love, truth and joy. With every moment's freely willed choice for the good, or the better, or the least bad alternative possible, a disciple receives more energy and impetus to make the next good choice. Every step taken on the path to holiness or integration puts you in a different place where a further attractive horizon begins to beckon. Positive transformations are inspired by the Spirit and are freely chosen responses. Goodness and virtue are simultaneously achievement and gift.

A woman opens herself to growth and change by focusing her attention on the things of God. Paul says to think of all things good, honorable, beautiful and noble. Why? Because what you pay attention to shapes the mind's consciousness and emotional responses. In sports psychology, athletes watch video images of expert performances over and over again in order to improve their own performance. Every other apprentice or student engages in the same repetitive focusing of attention. So too Christians will seek transformation through frequent acts of worship, prayer, Scripture reading and joyful celebrations. Love begets joyful hope, which in turn engenders merciful action that entrains cascading joy.

We may learn certain narrow lessons from pain about what not to do, but joy, love and happiness open us up to abundant creative living. Love and joy produce the trust that moves us to take more risks. Women's daring ventures continue. Christians are enticed to set sail farther and farther into the wider and deeper sea. Each woman finds her own unique passage over the waters. No one should ever court lethal storms and shipwrecks since it is against God's saving will for human flourishing. But when love, empathy and the effort to end suffering leads to suffering, hope for joy is not lost.

Women can grow in wisdom, love and joy throughout the most arduous of lives when they live in the presence of God. Hearts can rejoice and consciousness can expand through active love and mercy to others. Women traditionally have been able to give comfort, joy and pleasure.

CREATING NEW LIFE, NURTURING FAMILIES

Wives and mothers have nurtured their families as well as offering hospitality to those in their worlds. "Sisterhood is powerful" has been a slogan that points to social realities that still hold true. Women have always helped each other through times of trouble or need. In births, deaths, illness or conflict women have been able to bond and offer succor.

As some anthropological observers of early humans have noted: In dangerous crises females employ a "tend and befriend" strategy for survival. An individualistic "fight or flight" defense would abandon and endanger the children, so women make alliances with other females in order to protect themselves and their dependent children, strengthen kinship bonds, make alliances and create communal bonds. This strategy works for danger, but it also increases the intensity of life's celebration and joyful festivals. Women have always been creators of human happiness and hospitality. Providing food, comfort, shelter, counsel, friendship and endless cups of coffee and tea are concrete works of mercy. Hospitality is a core Christian virtue—even if is not the case that we entertain angels unawares. God loves a cheerful giver; and it is the case that those who give will receive far more than the measure they give.

The Spirit produces abundant fruit beyond our imagining. Direct individual sufferings will still come for Christian women, and empathy will bring more pain with the suffering of others. But love also brings joy and hope. The truth that Christian faith brings joy and happiness, no matter what suffering is encountered, is voiced in Christ's promises in the teachings known as the Beatitudes. Blessed, or deeply happy, are the poor, or those who mourn, or those who are persecuted for Christ's sake. They will be filled with comfort and joy. The sufferings of life are not illusions; they are truly painful but that is not the last word. In a disciple's life with God the presence of love both human and Divine, brings joy and fulfillment in the earthly journey. All the way to heaven is heaven, said the great Teresa of Ávila—who had her share of misery. With confidence that love brings joy and casts out fear, Christian women dare to make promises. They enter into loving marriages and become mothers. They may suffer much in family life, but they will also become transformed.

Women will fulfill the great scriptural words: "Although you have not seen him, you love him; and even though you do not see him now, you believe in him, you rejoice with an indescribable and glorious joy, for you are receiving the outcome of your faith, the salvation of your souls" (1Peter 1:8–9).

Food for Thought

1. Have your experiences of suffering come from different sources? Were times of suffering with others in empathy more beneficial than the misery that accompanied sinful and selfish behavior? How did you move through the suffering?
2. What experiences of joy have you had in your life? Did they seem to come from God and lead you to God?
3. Can you see ways that God has led you to become more like Christ through your experiences of suffering? And of joy? How did it happen?

Prayer

Invocation:
God of joy,
 Give us delight in your presence.
God of joy,
 Give us voices to praise your glory.
God of joy,
 Give us the power to give joy to others.

Scripture: Romans 8: 22–26

Response:
Let us pray for the Spirit to lift out hearts in love and joy:
   Bring the new creation to birth.
Let us pray for the Spirit to feel empathy with others who suffer:
   Bring the new creation to birth.
Let us pray for the Spirit to expand our hearts through suffering and joy,
   Bring the new creation to birth.

Prayer:
God of love help us to understand the birthing of the new creation in painful labor and joy. We ask for hope and trust in your loving power to bring all those in our human family to the new life in which every tear is wiped away. May the pain and suffering we experience be used to recreate the world. Amen.

• NOTES •

1. An accessible non-technical description of the new findings can be found in Daniel Goleman, *Social Intelligence: The Revolutionary New Science of Human Relationships* (New York: Bantam, 2007).
2. Daniel A. Keating, *Deification and Grace* (Naples, Fla.: Sapientia, 2007), p. 115.

• BIBLIOGRAPHY •

Callahan, Sidney. *Created for Joy: A Christian View of Suffering* (New York: Crossroad, 2007).

Crysdale, Cynthia S W. *Embracing Travail: Retrieving the Cross Today* (New York: Continuum, 1999).

Farley, Margaret. *Just Love: A Framework for Christian Sexual Ethics* (New York: Continuum, 2006).

Gaillardetz, Richard R. *A Daring Promise: A Spirituality of Christian Marriage* (New York: Crossroad, 2002).

Reynolds, Thomas E. *Vulnerable Communion: A Theology of Disability and Hospitality* (Grand Rapids: Brazos, 2008).

Whitehead, Evelyn Eaton and James D. *Marrying Well: Stages on the Journey of Christian Marriage* (Garden City, N. Y.: Doubleday, 1981).

Index

abstinence, sexual. *See* celibacy
addictions, and suffering, 104
adult children, caring for parents, 65–66
agape, as unconditional charity, 14
aging, and long-lasting marriage, 28–30
altruism
  and cooperation, 16–18
  through evolution, 19
  maternal, 67
annulment, 26
Augustine, and celibacy, 44

babies, playing with, 58
biblical scholarship, and teachings on marriage, 22–23

career women. *See* women, working
celibacy
  within marriage, 43–44
  seen as superior, 45–46
challenges
  with children, 3
  of sexual love, 50–52
  See also suffering
challenges, within marriage, 3, 30–34
  new, 26–27
  spiritual, 34–38
  women's, 21–22
change and growth, throughout life, 5–7
child abuse, 68
children
  challenges of, 3
  disabled, caring for, 93
  disappointment in, 65
  letting go of, 66
  not having more than one, for career purposes, 90, 92
  playing with, 58
  putting needs first, 94–95
children, raising
  by Christian standards, 64–65
  and good maternal thinking, 63
cocreators, women as, 2–3
communication
  and mothering, 56–57
  and nonverbal empathy, 72
community, work in, supportive nature of, 91–93
conflict resolution, 37
contempt, 38
conversion. *See* transformation
cooperation, and altruism, 16–18
creation
  and God's love, 101–102
  women as partners in, 2–3

dangers and obstacles, maternal, 66–69, 73
death, and suffering, 103
dementia, 107
depression, 66–67
deprivation, and suffering, 103
dialogue, within marriage, 37
dinner, eating together, 7
disabled, caring for, 93, 107
divorce
  causes and avoiding, 33–34
  culture of, 21
  See also annulment
domestic abuse, 25

eating together, 7
emotions
  destructive, 113
  and logic, interactions between, 18
  negative and positive, 110–111, 112–113
  shutting down, 105
  See also empathy, joy, love, suffering

empathy
 and human communication, 72
 for innocent and guilty, 107
 and suffering, 105–106
eros, 14
evolution
 and altruism, 19
 cultural and scientific, 17
 toward mothering, 56–59

family
 beginning, 28
 importance of conversation with, 7
 joys and challenges of, 5–7
 as milieu for transformation, 4–7
 See also children
family life, gifts of Holy Spirit as salvation of, 3
feminism
 and argument for career, 89–91
 reflecting on, 10
flow experiences, 86–87, 97
foresight, capacity for, 109–110

gay marriage. *See* same-sex marriage
glass ceilings, women breaking, 83
God
 and blessings of good and loving children, 71–72
 as love, 13
 love of, 14
 women as cocreators with, 2–3
 See also Jesus
gratitude list, 9, 10
growth
 during marriage, 41
 through sexual experience, 53
 See also transformation

happiness
 family as source, 8–9
 within marriage, 30–34
 See also joy
healing, in family life, 10

heroines, personal, 10
holidays, women's roles in, 9
Holy Spirit, fruits of, 3, 10
hope, and suffering, 110
hospitality, as core Christian virtue, 116
human communication
 and nonverbal empathy, 72
 research in, 56–57
human interdependence, 4–5
humor, in marriage, 39–40
husband, ideal, 96–97
"hyper-parenting," 68–69

income, and choosing whether to work, 89–91, 94

Jesus
 becoming more like, through suffering and joy, 117
 as man of sorrows and joy, 112
 taking up cross, 109
John Paul II, Pope, and attitudes on sex and marriage, 48
joy
 amid suffering, 108–110, 112–114
 and love, transformation through, 114–117
 and relation to God, 117
 and sadness, simultaneous, 112–113
 and suffering, 101–102
 wellsprings of, 110–112

laughter, in marriage, 39–40
Lewis, C.S., and divisions of love, 14
logic, and emotions, interactions between, 18
love, 13–19
 essence of, 15
 failure to, 19
 four distinct activities, 14
 for God and neighbor, 102
 individual capacities for, 19

and joy, transformation through, 114–117
maternal, 59–63
practicing, 7–10
unconditional, 62
See also marriage, sexual love

marriage, 21–22
celibacy in, 43–44
challenges of, 3
Christian, forces for and against, 40
Christian teaching on, 22–26
equality in, 22
fruits of, 39–40
gay. *See* same-sex marriage
as milieu for transformation, 4–7, 36–37
new thoughts and challenges, 26–27
saving, 34
spiritual challenges in, 34–38
stages and varieties, 28–34
welcome changes in attitudes, 47–50
See also family; relationships, complexity of
maternal dangers and obstacles, 66–69
maternal joy, and sexual joy, 14–15
maternal love, 59–63
maternal thinking, 63–66, 73
medical technology, and fertility, 22
mercy, Christian, reflected in mothering, 60
mother, as metaphor, 73
mother(s)
becoming, 55–56
stay-at-home, 91–94
suffering, 106–107
mothering
Christian affirmations of, 69–72
crucial nature of, 55
evolutionary preparation for, 56–59
and selflessness, 61–62

neighbor, love of, 14, 102

oxytocin, release of, 15

pain. *See* suffering
parents, adult children caring for, 65–66
Paul, Saint, and love, 16
perfectionism, in parenting, 70–71
philia, as activity of love, 14
polygamy, 26–27
post-partum depression, 66–67
power, and earning income, 89
prayer
for love, joy, and empathy, 118
for love and wisdom, 11
for marriage, 41–42
for meaningful work, 98–99
for mothering, 73–74
for self-knowledge, 19–20
for sexuality, 53
teaching children about, 71

relationships, complexity of, 6
research, in human communication, 56–57

same-sex marriage, 27
self, love of, 14
self-efficacy, as motivation, 86
selflessness, as natural result of motherhood, 61–62
sex
and modern culture, 47
obstacles to, 43–50
spouse's right to, 24–25
sex, attitudes toward
animalistic, 45–46
reflecting on, 52–53
welcome changes in, 47–50
sexual joy, and maternal joy, 14–15
sexual love, 50–52
social justice, working for, 80

spiritual challenges, in marriage, 34–38
storge, as activity of love, 14
suffering
   empathic, 105–108
   experiential, 117
   and joy, 101–102
   joy amid, 108–110, 112–114
   relieving, 105–106
   and taking up cross for Jesus' sake, 109
   thinking about, 102–104
support
   family and community, 91–93, 96
   for mothers, 64

talent
   as guide to choosing work, 80–81
   responsibility to use, 77–78
   taking seriously, 97
"tend and befriend" strategy, 116
Thérèse of Lisieux, Saint, 60
transformation
   communal nature of, 4–7
   through love and joy, 114–117
   within marriage, 36–37

Vatican II, and teaching on sex and marriage, 47
victimization, and suffering, 103–104
vocation, choosing, 80–84
volunteerism, as work, 84–85

"white marriages," 43
wife beating. *See* domestic abuse
wisdom, suffering leading to, 105
woman, sexual development as, 53
women
   busy roles of, 7–8
   and challenges of marriage, 21–22
   as cocreators with God, 2–3
   and growth, in face of hardship, 115–116
   self-giving practices of, 7, 10
   and sexuality, prejudices regarding, 45–47
women, working
   choosing to stop, 91–94
   Christian perspective on, 77–84
   feminist argument for, 89–91
   1950s attitude toward, 76–77
   and prioritization, 94–97
   psychological and experiential perspectives on, 84–88
women's rights
   and biblical scholarship, 22–24
   See also feminism
work
   choosing, 80–84
   Christian perspective on, 78–80
   defining, 84–86
   and family, conflicts, 98
   satisfying, 87–88
   women's. *See* women, working
workforce
   dropping out of, negative consequences of, 89
   reentering, 94

Called to Holiness Series

A groundbreaking eight-volume series on women's spirituality, *Called to Holiness: Spirituality for Catholic Women* will cover the many diverse facets of a woman's interior life and help her discover how God works with her and through her. An ideal resource for a woman seeking to find how God charges the moments of her life—from spirituality itself, to the spirituality of social justice, the spirituality of grieving the loss of a loved one, the creation and nurturing of families, the mentoring of young adult Catholic women, to recognition of the shared wisdom of women in the middle years—this series can be used by individuals or in groups. Far from the cloister or monastery, these books find God in the midst of a woman's everyday life and help her to find and celebrate God's presence day to day and acknowledge her own gifts as an ordinary "theologian." The books can be used independently or together for individual discussion or group faith sharing. Each book will include gathering rituals, reflection questions and annotated bibliographies.

Making Sense of God
A Woman's Perspective
Elizabeth A. Dreyer

The moment is ripe for ordinary Catholic women to "do Christian theology." Times such as these challenge us to be holy, to be alive in the Spirit, to summon the energy and make the commitment to help one another grow spiritually. Now is the time for Catholic women to make sense of God.

In this introductory volume to the *Called to Holiness* series, Catholic theologian Elizabeth Dreyer encourages us to acknowledge our dignity, harvest our gifts and empower all women in church and society. Dreyer helps us to shape what we think about God, justice, love, prayer, family life, the destiny of humanity and the entire universe.

Paper, 128 pp.
Order #B16884
ISBN 978-0-86716-884-6
$11.95

Living a Spirituality of Action
A Woman's Perspective
Joan Mueller

"Own your gifts and use them to make the world a better place," Catholic theologian Joan Mueller writes. In this practical book she provides us with ideas and encouragement to live and act with courage to change the world, even if our actions are sometimes small.

This is a book for all who hear about hungry people living in the park and decide to make sandwiches, who volunteer to teach children to read, who raise money to change systems that provide substandard care to the vulnerable, who can imagine a mothered world. Mueller invites us to discuss and embrace our shared wisdom.

Paper, 112 pp.
Order #B16885
ISBN 978-0-86716-885-3
$11.95

Grieving With Grace
A Woman's Perspective
Dolores R. Leckey

There are many ways in which the course of our daily lives can be altered—illness, change in residence, loss of employment and death of loved one. These alterations can require dramatic and even subtle changes in our everyday living, limit our options and force us to choose different priorities.

Dolores Leckey knows firsthand that the death of a spouse changes forever the rhythms of life at all levels—body, mind and soul. In this moving and personal narrative that includes entries from her journal, she shares with us her own shift in consciousness, in the way she sees God, herself and the world after her husband's death. She offers us consolation and hope.

Paper, 112 pp.
Order #B16888
ISBN 978-0-86716-888-4
$11.95

Awakening to Prayer
A Woman's Perspective
Clare Wagner

The word "prayer" is almost as generic as *food* or *book*, says Clare Wagner in *Awakening to Prayer: A Woman's Perspective*, and the varieties of prayer forms are countless. In this best and worst of times, Wagner writes, it is intriguing to ponder how women of the twenty-first century pray and enter into a relationship with Holy Presence.

To help us see anew, she draws on the wisdom of the Scriptures, the insights of the mystics and the experience of ordinary, vibrant women and men living in our midst. She offers suggestions of words to use and rituals to experience to help us awaken to prayer.

Paper, 112 pp.
Order #B16892
ISBN 978-0-86716-892-1
$11.95

Embracing Latina Spirituality
A Woman's Perspective
Michelle A. Gonzalez

Latinas treat the sacred in ways that are similar to the ways we treat those we encounter every day: They converse with statues of saints and Mary, leave them flowers and light candles to persuade them to gain favor for us, and become angry when prayers are not answered. These everyday aspects of Latina spirituality reflect a strong sense of family and community that we can embrace as a refreshing spiritual alternative to the individualism that permeates our society.

Entering into the world of Latina spirituality offers new ways to understand self and community and to approach prayer, diversity and the struggle against oppression. Latina spirituality provides us an entry point into true unity.

Paper, 112 pp.
Order #B16886
ISBN 978-0-86716-886-0
$11.95

Finding My Voice
A Young Woman's Perspective
Beth M. Knobbe

Finding My Voice: A Young Woman's Perspective will help you find answers to life's persistent questions: Who am I? Is God in my life? What does God want me to do?

Beth M. Knobbe understands firsthand the ups and downs of being twenty-something, the desire to belong, the longing to love and be loved. She knows the mysteries and realities of getting a career off the ground, the subtle temptations to conform to what the world wants and the ads say you must be, and the challenges you face to make people understand that you have a voice and you have something meaningful to say.

Paper, 160 pp.
Order #B16894
ISBN 978-0-86716-894-5
$11.95

About the Author

Sidney Callahan, PH.D., author, scholar and licensed psychologist, earned her B.A. in English from Bryn Mawr College, her M.A. in psychology from Sarah Lawrence College and a PH.D. in social and personality psychology from the City University of New York. She has written books, articles and columns devoted to religious, psychological and ethical questions. She has been a tenured professor of psychology and held visiting chairs of moral theology and psychology at Georgetown University and St. John's University in New York. She is a Distinguished Scholar at The Hastings Center. She and Daniel Callahan have been married since 1954 and have six children and five grandchildren.